THE TALES OF TCHEHOV

VOL. IX
THE SCHOOLMISTRESS
AND OTHER STORIES

THE
SCHOOLMISTRESS
AND OTHER STORIES

BY

ANTON TCHEHOV

FROM THE RUSSIAN
BY CONSTANCE GARNETT

LONDON
CHATTO & WINDUS
1920

CONTENTS

CONTENTS

THE SCHOOLMISTRESS

clearly. Her past was like her present was here,
and she could imagine no other future than the
school, the road to the town and back again, and
again the school and again the road . . . .
She had lost the habit of thinking of her
past before she became a schoolmistress, and had
almost forgotten it. She had once had a father
and mother; they lived in Moscow in a big
flat

THE SCHOOLMISTRESS

At half-past eight they drove out of the town.

The highroad was dry, a lovely April sun was
shining warmly, but the snow was still lying in
the ditches and in the woods. Winter, dark, long,
and spiteful, was hardly over; spring had come
all of a sudden. But neither the warmth nor the
languid transparent woods, warmed by the breath
of spring, nor the black flocks of birds flying over
the huge puddles that were like lakes, nor the
marvellous fathomless sky, into which it seemed
one would have gone away so joyfully, presented
anything new or interesting to Marya Vassilyevna,
who was sitting in the cart. For thirteen years
she had been schoolmistress, and there was
no reckoning how many times during all those
years she had been to the town for her salary; and
whether it were spring as now, or a rainy autumn
evening, or winter, it was all the same to her,
and she always—invariably—longed for one thing
only, to get to the end of her journey as quickly
as could be.

She felt as though she had been living in that
part of the country for ages and ages, for a hundred
years, and it seemed to her that she knew every
stone, every tree on the road from the town to her

school. Her past was here, her present was here, and she could imagine no other future than the school, the road to the town and back again, and again the school and again the road. . . .

She had got out of the habit of thinking of her past before she became a schoolmistress, and had almost forgotten it. She had once had a father and mother; they had lived in Moscow in a big flat near the Red Gate, but of all that life there was left in her memory only something vague and fluid like a dream. Her father had died when she was ten years old, and her mother had died soon after. . . . She had a brother, an officer; at first they used to write to each other, then her brother had given up answering her letters, he had got out of the way of writing. Of her old belongings, all that was left was a photograph of her mother, but it had grown dim from the dampness of the school, and now nothing could be seen but the hair and the eyebrows.

When they had driven a couple of miles, old Semyon, who was driving, turned round and said:

" They have caught a government clerk in the town. They have taken him away. The story is that with some Germans he killed Alexeyev, the Mayor, in Moscow."

" Who told you that ?"

" They were reading it in the paper, in Ivan Ionov's tavern."

And again they were silent for a long time. Marya Vassilyevna thought of her school, of the examination that was coming soon, and of the girl and four boys she was sending up for it. And just as she was thinking about the examination, she was overtaken by a neighbouring landowner called Hanov in a carriage with four horses, the very man who had been examiner in her school the year before. When he came up to her he recognized her and bowed.

" Good-morning," he said to her. " You are driving home, I suppose."

This Hanov, a man of forty with a listless expression and a face that showed signs of wear, was beginning to look old, but was still handsome and admired by women. He lived in his big homestead alone, and was not in the service; and people used to say of him that he did nothing at home but walk up and down the room whistling, or play chess with his old footman. People said, too, that he drank heavily. And indeed at the examination the year before the very papers he brought with him smelt of wine and scent. He had been dressed all in new clothes on that occasion, and Marya Vassilyevna thought him very attractive, and all the while she sat beside him she had felt embarrassed. She was accustomed to see frigid and sensible examiners at the school, while this one did not remember a single prayer, or know what to ask questions about, and was exceedingly courteous and delicate, giving nothing but the highest marks.

" I am going to visit Bakvist," he went on, addressing Marya Vassilyevna, " but I am told he is not at home."

They turned off the highroad into a by-road to the village, Hanov leading the way and

Semyon following. The four horses moved at a walking pace, with effort dragging the heavy carriage through the mud. Semyon tacked from side to side, keeping to the edge of the road, at one time through a snowdrift, at another through a pool, often jumping out of the cart and helping the horse. Marya Vassilyevna was still thinking about the school, wondering whether the arithmetic questions at the examination would be difficult or easy. And she felt annoyed with the Zemstvo board at which she had found no one the day before. How unbusiness-like! Here she had been asking them for the last two years to dismiss the watchman, who did nothing, was rude to her, and hit the schoolboys; but no one paid any attention. It was hard to find the president at the office, and when one did find him he would say with tears in his eyes that he hadn't a moment to spare; the inspector visited the school at most once in three years, and knew nothing whatever about his work, as he had been in the Excise Duties Department, and had received the post of school inspector through influence. The School Council met very rarely, and there was no knowing where it met; the school guardian was an almost illiterate peasant, the head of a tanning business, unintelligent, rude, and a great friend of the watchman's— and goodness knows to whom she could appeal with complaints or enquiries. . . .

" He really is handsome," she thought, glancing at Hanov.

The road grew worse and worse. . . . They drove into the wood. Here there was no room to turn round, the wheels sank deeply in, water splashed and gurgled through them, and sharp twigs struck them in the face.

"What a road!" said Hanov, and he laughed.

The schoolmistress looked at him and could not understand why this queer man lived here. What could his money, his interesting appearance, his refined bearing do for him here, in this mud, in this God-forsaken, dreary place? He got no special advantages out of life, and here, like Semyon, was driving at a jog-trot on an appalling road and enduring the same discomforts. Why live here if one could live in Petersburg or abroad? And one would have thought it would be nothing for a rich man like him to make a good road instead of this bad one, to avoid enduring this misery and seeing the despair on the faces of his coachman and Semyon; but he only laughed, and apparently did not mind, and wanted no better life. He was kind, soft, naïve, and he did not understand this coarse life, just as at the examination he did not know the prayers. He subscribed nothing to the schools but globes, and genuinely regarded himself as a useful person and a prominent worker in the cause of popular education. And what use were his globes here?

"Hold on, Vassilyevna!" said Semyon.

The cart lurched violently and was on the point of upsetting; something heavy rolled on to Marya Vassilyevna's feet—it was her parcel of purchases. There was a steep ascent uphill through the clay; here in the winding ditches rivulets were gurgling. The water seemed to have gnawed away the road;

and how could one get along here ! The horses breathed hard. Hanov got out of his carriage and walked at the side of the road in his long over-coat. He was hot.

"What a road!" he said, and laughed again. "It would soon smash up one's carriage."

"Nobody obliges you to drive about in such weather," said Semyon surlily. "You should stay at home."

"I am dull at home, grandfather. I don't like staying at home."

Beside old Semyon he looked graceful and vigorous, but yet in his walk there was something just perceptible which betrayed in him a being already touched by decay, weak, and on the road to ruin. And all at once there was a whiff of spirits in the wood. Marya Vassilyevna was filled with dread and pity for this man going to his ruin for no visible cause or reason, and it came into her mind that if she had been his wife or sister she would have devoted her whole life to saving him from ruin. His wife ! Life was so ordered that here he was living in his great house alone, and she was living in a God-forsaken village alone, and yet for some reason the mere thought that he and she might be close to one another and equals seemed impossible and absurd. In reality, life was arranged and human relations were com-plicated so utterly beyond all understanding that when one thought about it one felt uncanny and one's heart sank.

"And it is beyond all understanding," she thought, "why God gives beauty, this graciousness, and sad, sweet eyes, to weak, unlucky, useless people—why they are so charming."

"Here we must turn off to the right," said Hanov, getting into his carriage. "Good-bye! I wish you all things good!"

And again she thought of her pupils, of the examination, of the watchman, of the School Council; and when the wind brought the sound of the retreating carriage these thoughts were mingled with others. She longed to think of beautiful eyes, of love, of the happiness which would never be. . . .

His wife? It was cold in the morning, there was no one to heat the stove, the watchman disappeared; the children came in as soon as it was light, bringing in snow and mud and making a noise: it was all so inconvenient, so comfortless. Her abode consisted of one little room and the kitchen close by. Her head ached every day after her work, and after dinner she had heartburn. She had to collect money from the schoolchildren for wood and for the watchman, and to give it to the school guardian, and then to entreat him—that overfed, insolent peasant—for God's sake to send her wood. And at night she dreamed of examinations, peasants, snowdrifts. And this life was making her grow old and coarse, making her ugly, angular, and awkward, as though she were made of lead. She was always afraid, and she would get up from her seat and not venture to sit down in the presence of a member of the Zemstvo or the school guardian. And she used formal, deferential expressions when she spoke of any one of them. And no one thought her attractive, and life was passing drearily, without affection, without friendly sympathy, without interesting acquaintances. How awful it would have been in her position if she had fallen in love !

" Hold on, Vassilyevna !"

Again a sharp ascent uphill. . . .

She had become a schoolmistress from necessity, without feeling any vocation for it; and she had never thought of a vocation, of serving the cause of enlightenment; and it always seemed to her that what was most important in her work was not the children, nor enlightenment, but the examinations. And what time had she for thinking of vocation, of serving the cause of enlightenment ? Teachers, badly paid doctors, and their assistants, with their terribly hard work, have not even the comfort of thinking that they are serving an idea or the people, as their heads are always stuffed with thoughts of their daily bread, of wood for the fire, of bad roads, of illnesses. It is a hard-working, an uninteresting life, and only silent, patient cart-horses like Marya Vassilyevna could put up with it for long; the lively, nervous, impressionable people who talked about a vocation and serving the idea were soon weary of it and gave up the work.

Semyon kept picking out the driest and shortest way, first by a meadow, then by the backs of the village huts; but in one place the peasants would not let them pass, in another it was the priest's land and they could not cross it, in another Ivan Ionov had bought a plot from the landowner and had dug a ditch round it. They kept having to turn back.

They reached Nizhneye Gorodistche. Near the tavern on the dung-strewn earth, where the snow was still lying, there stood waggons that had brought great bottles of crude sulphuric acid. There were a great many people in the tavern, all drivers, and there was a smell of vodka, tobacco, and sheepskins. There was a loud noise of conversation and the banging of the swing-door. Through the wall, without ceasing for a moment, came the sound of a concertina being played in the shop. Marya Vassilyevna sat down and drank some tea, while at the next table peasants were drinking vodka and beer, perspiring from the tea they had just swallowed and the stifling fumes of the tavern.

"I say, Kuzma!" voices kept shouting in confusion. "What there!" "The Lord bless us!" "Ivan Dementyitch, I can tell you that!" "Look out, old man!"

A little pock-marked man with a black beard, who was quite drunk, was suddenly surprised by something and began using bad language.

"What are you swearing at, you there?" Semyon, who was sitting some way off, responded angrily. "Don't you see the young lady?"

"The young lady!" someone mimicked in another corner.

"Swinish crow!"

"We meant nothing . . ." said the little man in confusion. "I beg your pardon. We pay with our money and the young lady with hers. Good-morning!"

"Good-morning," answered the schoolmistress.

"And we thank you most feelingly."

Marya Vassilyevna drank her tea with satisfaction, and she, too, began turning red like the peasants, and fell to thinking again about firewood, about the watchman. . . .

"Stay, old man," she heard from the next table, "it's the schoolmistress from Vyazovye. . . . We know her; she's a good young lady."

"She's all right!"

The swing-door was continually banging, some coming in, others going out. Marya Vassilyevna sat on, thinking all the time of the same things, while the concertina went on playing and playing. The patches of sunshine had been on the floor, then they passed to the counter, to the wall, and disappeared altogether; so by the sun it was past midday. The peasants at the next table were getting ready to go. The little man, somewhat unsteadily, went up to Marya Vassilyevna and held out his hand to her; following his example, the others shook hands, too, at parting, and went out one after another, and the swing-door squeaked and slammed nine times.

"Vassilyevna, get ready," Semyon called to her.

They set off. And again they went at a walking pace.

"A little while back they were building a school here in their Nizhneye Gorodistche," said Semyon, turning round. "It was a wicked thing that was done!"

"Why, what?"

"They say the president put a thousand in his

pocket, and the school guardian another thousand in his, and the teacher five hundred."

"The whole school only cost a thousand. It's wrong to slander people, grandfather. That's all nonsense."

"I don't know, . . . I only tell you what folks say."

But it was clear that Semyon did not believe the schoolmistress. The peasants did not believe her. They always thought she received too large a salary, twenty-one roubles a month (five would have been enough), and that of the money that she collected from the children for the firewood and the watchman the greater part she kept for herself. The guardian thought the same as the peasants, and he himself made a profit off the firewood and received payments from the peasants for being a guardian—without the knowledge of the authorities.

The forest, thank God! was behind them, and now it would be flat, open ground all the way to Vyazovye, and there was not far to go now. They had to cross the river and then the railway line, and then Vyazovye was in sight.

"Where are you driving?" Marya Vassilyevna asked Semyon. "Take the road to the right to the bridge."

"Why, we can go this way as well. It's not deep enough to matter."

"Mind you don't drown the horse."

"What?"

"Look, Hanov is driving to the bridge," said Marya Vassilyevna, seeing the four horses far away to the right. "It is he, I think."

"It is. So he didn't find Bakvist at home. What a pig-headed fellow he is. Lord have mercy upon us! He's driven over there, and what for? It's fully two miles nearer this way."

They reached the river. In the summer it was a little stream easily crossed by wading. It usually dried up in August, but now, after the spring floods, it was a river forty feet in breadth, rapid, muddy, and cold; on the bank and right up to the water there were fresh tracks of wheels, so it had been crossed here.

"Go on!" shouted Semyon angrily and anxiously, tugging violently at the reins and jerking his elbows as a bird does its wings. "Go on!"

The horse went on into the water up to his belly and stopped, but at once went on again with an effort, and Marya Vassilyevna was aware of a keen chilliness in her feet.

"Go on!" she, too, shouted, getting up. "Go on!"

They got out on the bank.

"Nice mess it is, Lord have mercy upon us!" muttered Semyon, setting straight the harness. "It's a perfect plague with this Zemstvo. . . ."

Her shoes and goloshes were full of water, the lower part of her dress and of her coat and one sleeve were wet and dripping: the sugar and flour had got wet, and that was worst of all, and Marya Vassilyevna could only clasp her hands in despair and say:

"Oh, Semyon, Semyon! How tiresome you are, really! . . ."

The barrier was down at the railway crossing.

A train was coming out of the station. Marya
Vassilyevna stood at the crossing waiting till it
should pass, and shivering all over with cold.
Vyazovye was in sight now, and the school with
the green roof, and the church with its crosses
flashing in the evening sun: and the station windows flashed too, and a pink smoke rose from the
engine . . . and it seemed to her that everything
was trembling with cold.

Here was the train; the windows reflected the
gleaming light like the crosses on the church: it
made her eyes ache to look at them. On the little
platform between two first-class carriages a lady
was standing, and Marya Vassilyevna glanced at
her as she passed. Her mother! What a resem-
blance! Her mother had had just such luxuriant
hair, just such a brow and bend of the head. And
with amazing distinctness, for the first time in
those thirteen years, there rose before her mind a
vivid picture of her mother, her father, her brother,
their flat in Moscow, the aquarium with little
fish, everything to the tiniest detail; she heard the
sound of the piano, her father's voice; she felt
as she had been then, young, good-looking, well-
dressed, in a bright warm room among her own
people. A feeling of joy and happiness suddenly
came over her, she pressed her hands to her
temples in an ecstacy, and called softly, beseech-
ingly:

" Mother !"

And she began crying, she did not know why.
Just at that instant Hanov drove up with his team
of four horses, and seeing him she imagined happi-

ness such as she had never had, and smiled and
nodded to him as an equal and a friend, and it
seemed to her that her happiness, her triumph,
was glowing in the sky and on all sides, in the
windows and on the trees. Her father and mother
had never died, she had never been a schoolmistress, it was a long, tedious, strange dream,
and now she had awakened. . . .

"Vassilyevna, get in!"

And at once it all vanished. The barrier was
slowly raised. Marya Vassilyevna, shivering and
numb with cold, got into the cart. The carriage
with the four horses crossed the railway line;
Semyon followed it. The signalman took off
his cap.

"And here is Vyazovye. Here we are."

A NERVOUS BREAKDOWN

A NERVOUS BREAKDOWN

I.

A MEDICAL student called Mayer, and a pupil of the Moscow School of Painting, Sculpture, and Architecture called Rybnikov, went one evening to see their friend Vassilyev, a law student, and suggested that he should go with them to S. Street. For a long time Vassilyev would not consent to go, but in the end he put on his great-coat and went with them.

He knew nothing of fallen women except by hearsay and from books, and he had never in his life been in the houses in which they live. He knew that there are immoral women who, under the pressure of fatal circumstances—environment, bad education, poverty, and so on—are forced to sell their honour for money. They know nothing of pure love, have no children, have no civil rights; their mothers and sisters weep over them as though they were dead, science treats of them as an evil, men address them with contemptuous familiarity. But in spite of all that, they do not lose the semblance and image of God. They all acknowledge their sin and hope for salvation. Of the means that lead to salvation they can avail themselves to the fullest extent. Society, it is true, will not forgive

people their past, but in the sight of God St. Mary
of Egypt is no lower than the other saints. When
it had happened to Vassilyev in the street to
recognize a fallen woman as such, by her dress or
her manners, or to see a picture of one in a comic
paper, he always remembered a story he had once
read : a young man, pure and self-sacrificing,
loves a fallen woman and urges her to become his
wife; she, considering herself unworthy of such
happiness, takes poison.

Vassilyev lived in one of the side streets turning
out of Tverskoy Boulevard. When he came out
of the house with his two friends it was about
eleven o'clock. The first snow had not long
fallen, and all nature was under the spell of the
fresh snow. There was the smell of snow in the air,
the snow crunched softly under the feet; the earth,
the roofs, the trees, the seats on the boulevard,
everything was soft, white, young, and this made
the houses look quite different from the day
before; the street lamps burned more brightly, the
air was more transparent, the carriages rumbled
with a deeper note, and with the fresh, light, frosty
air a feeling stirred in the soul akin to the white,
youthful, feathery snow. " Against my will an
unseen force," hummed the medical student in
his agreeable tenor, " has led me to these mournful
shores."

" Behold the mill . . ." the artist seconded
him, " in ruins now. . . ."

" Behold the mill . . . in ruins now," the
medical student repeated, raising his eyebrows and
shaking his head mournfully.

He paused, rubbed his forehead, trying to remember the words, and then sang aloud, so well that passers-by looked round:

> "Here in old days when I was free,
> Love, free, unfettered, greeted me."

The three of them went into a restaurant and, without taking off their greatcoats, drank a couple of glasses of vodka each. Before drinking the second glass, Vassilyev noticed a bit of cork in his vodka, raised the glass to his eyes, and gazed into it for a long time, screwing up his shortsighted eyes. The medical student did not understand his expression, and said:

"Come, why look at it? No philosophizing, please. Vodka is given us to be drunk, sturgeon to be eaten, women to be visited, snow to be walked upon. For one evening anyway live like a human being!"

"But I haven't said anything . . ." said Vassilyev, laughing. "Am I refusing to?"

There was a warmth inside him from the vodka. He looked with softened feelings at his friends, admired them and envied them. In these strong, healthy, cheerful people how wonderfully balanced everything is, how finished and smooth is everything in their minds and souls! They sing, and have a passion for the theatre, and draw, and talk a great deal, and drink, and they don't have headaches the day after; they are both poetical and debauched, both soft and hard; they can work, too, and be indignant, and laugh without reason, and talk nonsense; they are warm, honest, self-sacrificing, and as men are in no way inferior to himself, Vassilyev, who watched over every step he took and every word he uttered, who was fastidious and cautious, and ready to raise every trifle to the level of a problem. And he longed for one evening to live as his friends did, to open out, to let himself loose from his own control. If vodka had to be drunk, he would drink it, though his head would be splitting next morning. If he were taken to the women he would go. He would laugh, play the fool, gaily respond to the passing advances of strangers in the street. . . .

He went out of the restaurant laughing. He liked his friends—one in a crushed broad-brimmed hat, with an affectation of artistic untidiness; the other in a sealskin cap, a man not poor, though he affected to belong to the Bohemia of learning. He liked the snow, the pale street lamps, the sharp black tracks left in the first snow by the feet of the passers-by. He liked the air, and especially that limpid, tender, naïve, as it were virginal tone, which can be seen in nature only twice in the year —when everything is covered with snow, and in spring on bright days and moonlight evenings when the ice breaks on the river.

> "Against my will an unknown force,
> Has led me to these mournful shores."

he hummed in an undertone.

And the tune for some reason haunted him and his friends all the way, and all three of them hummed it mechanically, not in time with one another.

Vassilyev's imagination was picturing how, in another ten minutes, he and his friends would knock at a door; how by little dark passages and dark rooms they would steal in to the women; how, taking advantage of the darkness, he would strike a match, would light up and see the face of a martyr and a guilty smile. The unknown, fair or dark, would certainly have her hair down and be wearing a white dressing-jacket; she would be panic-stricken by the light, would be fearfully confused, and would say: "For God's sake, what are you doing! Put it out!" It would all be dreadful, but interesting and new.

II.

The friends turned out of Trubnoy Square into Gratchevka, and soon reached the side street which Vassilyev only knew by reputation. Seeing two rows of houses with brightly lighted windows and wide-open doors, and hearing gay strains of pianos and violins, sounds which floated out from every door and mingled in a strange chaos, as though an unseen orchestra were tuning up in the darkness above the roofs, Vassilyev was surprised and said:

"What a lot of houses!"

"That's nothing," said the medical student. "In London there are ten times as many. There are about a hundred thousand such women there."

The cabmen were sitting on their boxes as calmly and indifferently as in any other side street; the same passers-by were walking along the pavement as in other streets. No one was hurrying, no one was hiding his face in his coat-collar, no one shook his head reproachfully. . . . And in this indifference to the noisy chaos of pianos and violins, to the bright windows and wide-open doors, there was a feeling of something very open, insolent, reckless, and devil-may-care. Probably it was as gay and noisy at the slave-markets in their day, and people's faces and movements showed the same indifference.

"Let us begin from the beginning," said the artist.

The friends went into a narrow passage lighted by a lamp with a reflector. When they opened the door a man in a black coat, with an unshaven face like a flunkey's, and sleepy-looking eyes, got up lazily from a yellow sofa in the hall. The place smelt like a laundry with an odour of vinegar in addition. A door from the hall led into a brightly lighted room. The medical student and the artist stopped at this door and, craning their necks, peeped into the room.

"Buona sera, signori, rigolleto—hugenotti—traviata!" began the artist, with a theatrical bow.

"Havanna—tarakano—pistoleto!" said the medical student, pressing his cap to his breast and bowing low.

Vassilyev was standing behind them. He would have liked to make a theatrical bow and say something silly, too, but he only smiled, felt an awkwardness that was like shame, and waited impatiently for what would happen next.

A little fair girl of seventeen or eighteen, with

short hair, in a short light-blue frock with a bunch of white ribbon on her bosom, appeared in the doorway.

"Why do you stand at the door?" she said. "Take off your coats and come into the drawing-room."

The medical student and the artist, still talking Italian, went into the drawing-room. Vassilyev followed them irresolutely.

"Gentlemen, take off your coats!" the flunkey said sternly; "you can't go in like that."

In the drawing-room there was, besides the girl, another woman, very stout and tall, with a foreign face and bare arms. She was sitting near the piano, laying out a game of patience on her lap. She took no notice whatever of the visitors.

"Where are the other young ladies?" asked the medical student.

"They are having their tea," said the fair girl. "Stepan," she called, "go and tell the young ladies some students have come!"

A little later a third young lady came into the room. She was wearing a bright red dress with blue stripes. Her face was painted thickly and unskilfully, her brow was hidden under her hair, and there was an unblinking, frightened stare in her eyes. As she came in, she began at once singing some song in a coarse, powerful contralto. After her a fourth appeared, and after her a fifth. . . .

In all this Vassilyev saw nothing new or interesting. It seemed to him that that room, the piano, the looking-glass in its cheap gilt frame, the bunch of white ribbon, the dress with the blue stripes, and the blank indifferent faces, he had seen before and more than once. Of the darkness, the silence, the secrecy, the guilty smile, of all that he had expected to meet here and had dreaded, he saw no trace.

Everything was ordinary, prosaic, and uninteresting. Only one thing faintly stirred his curiosity—the terrible, as it were intentionally designed, bad taste which was visible in the cornices, in the absurd pictures, in the dresses, in the bunch of ribbons. There was something characteristic and peculiar in this bad taste.

" How poor and stupid it all is !" thought Vassilyev. " What is there in all this trumpery I see now that can tempt a normal man and excite him to commit the horrible sin of buying a human being for a rouble ? I understand any sin for the sake of splendour, beauty, grace, passion, taste; but what is there here ? What is there here worth sinning for ? But . . . one mustn't think !"

" Beardy, treat me to some porter !" said the fair girl, addressing him.

Vassilyev was at once overcome with confusion.

" With pleasure," he said, bowing politely. " Only excuse me, madam, I . . . I won't drink with you. I don't drink."

Five minutes later the friends went off into another house.

" Why did you ask for porter ?" said the medical student angrily. " What a millionaire ! You have thrown away six roubles for no reason whatever—simply waste !"

"If she wants it, why not let her have the pleasure?" said Vassilyev, justifying himself.

"You did not give pleasure to her, but to the 'Madam.' They are told to ask the visitors to stand them treat because it is a profit to the keeper."

"Behold the mill. . . ." hummed the artist, "in ruins now. . . ."

Going into the next house, the friends stopped in the hall and did not go into the drawing-room. Here, as in the first house, a figure in a black coat, with a sleepy face like a flunkey's, got up from a sofa in the hall. Looking at this flunkey, at his face and his shabby black coat, Vassilyev thought: "What must an ordinary simple Russian have gone through before fate flung him down as a flunkey here? Where had he been before and what had he done? What was awaiting him? Was he married? Where was his mother, and did she know that he was a servant here?" And Vassilyev could not help particularly noticing the flunkey in each house. In one of the houses— he thought it was the fourth—there was a little spare, frail-looking flunkey with a watchchain on his waistcoat. He was reading a newspaper, and took no notice of them when they went in. Looking at his face, Vassilyev, for some reason, thought that a man with such a face might steal, might murder, might bear false witness. But the face was really interesting: a big forehead, grey eyes, a little flattened nose, thin compressed lips, and a blankly stupid and at the same time insolent expression like that of a young harrier overtaking a hare. Vassilyev thought it would be nice to touch this man's hair, to see whether it was soft or coarse. It must be coarse like a dog's.

III.

Having drunk two glasses of porter, the artist became suddenly tipsy and grew unnaturally lively.

"Let's go to another!" he said peremptorily, waving his hands. "I will take you to the best one."

When he had brought his friends to the house which in his opinion was the best, he declared his firm intention of dancing a quadrille. The medical student grumbled something about their having to pay the musicians a rouble, but agreed to be his *vis-à-vis*. They began dancing.

It was just as nasty in the best house as in the worst. Here there were just the same looking-glasses and pictures, the same styles of coiffure and dress. Looking round at the furnishing of the rooms and the costumes, Vassilyev realized that this was not lack of taste, but something that might be called the taste, and even the style, of S. Street, which could not be found elsewhere —something intentional in its ugliness, not accidental, but elaborated in the course of years. After he had been in eight houses he was no longer surprised at the colour of the dresses, at the long trains, the gaudy ribbons, the sailor dresses, and the thick purplish rouge on the cheeks; he saw that it all had to be like this, that if a single one of the women had been dressed like a human being, or if there had been one decent engraving on the wall, the general tone of the whole street would have suffered.

"How unskilfully they sell themselves!" he thought. "How can they fail to understand that vice is only alluring when it is beautiful and hidden, when it wears the mask of virtue? Modest black dresses, pale faces, mournful smiles, and darkness would be far more effective than this clumsy tawdriness. Stupid things! If they don't understand it of themselves, their visitors might surely have taught them. . . ."

A young lady in a Polish dress edged with white fur came up to him and sat down beside him.

"You nice dark man, why aren't you dancing?" she asked. "Why are you so dull?"

"Because it is dull."

"Treat me to some Lafitte. Then it won't be dull."

Vassilyev made no answer. He was silent for a little, and then asked:

"What time do you get to sleep?"

"At six o'clock."

"And what time do you get up?"

"Sometimes at two and sometimes at three."

"And what do you do when you get up?"

"We have coffee, and at six o'clock we have dinner."

"And what do you have for dinner?"

"Usually soup, beefsteak, and dessert. Our madam keeps the girls well. But why do you ask all this?"

" Oh, just to talk. . . ."

Vassilyev longed to talk to the young lady about many things. He felt an intense desire to find out where she came from, whether her parents were living, and whether they knew that she was here; how she had come into this house; whether she were cheerful and satisfied, or sad and oppressed by gloomy thoughts; whether she hoped some day to get out of her present position. . . . But he could not think how to begin or in what shape to put his questions so as not to seem impertinent. He thought for a long time, and asked:

" How old are you ?"

" Eighty," the young lady jested, looking with a laugh at the antics of the artist as he danced.

All at once she burst out laughing at something, and uttered a long cynical sentence loud enough to be heard by everyone. Vassilyev was aghast, and not knowing how to look, gave a constrained smile. He was the only one who smiled; all the others, his friends, the musicians, the women, did not even glance towards his neighbour, but seemed not to have heard her.

" Stand me some Lafitte," his neighbour said again.

Vassilyev felt a repulsion for her white fur and for her voice, and walked away from her. It seemed to him hot and stifling, and his heart began throbbing slowly but violently, like a hammer— one ! two ! three !

" Let us go away !" he said, pulling the artist by his sleeve.

" Wait a little ; let me finish."

While the artist and the medical student were

finishing the quadrille, to avoid looking at the women, Vassilyev scrutinized the musicians. A respectable-looking old man in spectacles, rather like Marshal Bazaine, was playing the piano; a young man with a fair beard, dressed in the latest fashion, was playing the violin. The young man had a face that did not look stupid nor exhausted, but intelligent, youthful, and fresh. He was dressed fancifully and with taste; he played with feeling. It was a mystery how he and the respectable-looking old man had come here. How was it they were not ashamed to sit here? What were they thinking about when they looked at the women?

If the violin and the piano had been played by men in rags, looking hungry, gloomy, drunken, with dissipated or stupid faces, then one could have understood their presence, perhaps. As it was, Vassilyev could not understand it at all. He recalled the story of the fallen woman he had once read, and he thought now that that human figure with the guilty smile had nothing in common with what he was seeing now. It seemed to him that he was seeing not fallen women, but some different world quite apart, alien to him and incomprehensible; if he had seen this world before on the stage, or read of it in a book, he would not have believed in it. . . .

The woman with the white fur burst out laughing again and uttered a loathsome sentence in a loud voice. A feeling of disgust took possession of him. He flushed crimson and went out of the room.

"Wait a minute, we are coming too!" the artist shouted to him.

IV.

"While we were dancing," said the medical student, as they all three went out into the street, "I had a conversation with my partner. We talked about her first romance. He, the hero, was an accountant at Smolensk with a wife and five children. She was seventeen, and she lived with her papa and mamma, who sold soap and candles."

"How did he win her heart?" asked Vassilyev.

"By spending fifty roubles on underclothes for her. What next!"

"So he knew how to get his partner's story out of her," thought Vassilyev about the medical student. "But I don't know how to."

"I say, I am going home!" he said.

"What for?"

"Because I don't know how to behave here. Besides, I am bored, disgusted. What is there amusing in it? If they were human beings—but they are savages and animals. I am going; do as you like."

"Come, Grisha, Grigory, darling . . ." said the artist in a tearful voice, hugging Vassilyev, "come along! Let's go to one more together and damnation take them! . . . Please do, Grisha!"

They persuaded Vassilyev and led him up a staircase. In the carpet and the gilt banisters, in the porter who opened the door, and in the panels that decorated the hall, the same S. Street style was apparent, but carried to a greater perfection, more imposing.

" I really will go home !" said Vassilyev as he was taking off his coat.

"Come, come, dear boy," said the artist, and he kissed him on the neck. " Don't be tiresome. . . . Gri-gri, be a good comrade ! We came together, we will go back together. What a beast you are, really !"

" I can wait for you in the street. I think it's loathsome, really !"

"Come, come, Grisha. . . . If it is loathsome, you can observe it ! Do you understand ? You can observe !"

"One must take an objective view of things," said the medical student gravely.

Vassilyev went into the drawing-room and sat down. There were a number of visitors in the room besides him and his friends: two infantry officers, a bald, grey-haired gentleman in spectacles, two beardless youths from the institute of land-surveying, and a very tipsy man who looked like an actor. All the young ladies were taken up with these visitors and paid no attention to Vassilyev.

Only one of them, dressed *à la Aida*, glanced sideways at him, smiled, and said, yawning: " A dark one has come. . . ."

Vassilyev's heart was throbbing and his face burned. He felt ashamed before these visitors of his presence here, and he felt disgusted and miserable. He was tormented by the thought that he, a decent and loving man (such as he had hitherto considered himself), hated these women and felt nothing but repulsion towards them. He

IX.

3

felt pity neither for the women nor the musicians nor the flunkeys.

"It is because I am not trying to understand them," he thought. "They are all more like animals than human beings, but of course they are human beings all the same, they have souls. One must understand them and then judge. . . ."

"Grisha, don't go, wait for us," the artist shouted to him and disappeared.

The medical student disappeared soon after.

"Yes, one must make an effort to understand, one mustn't be like this . . ." Vassilyev went on thinking.

And he began gazing at each of the women with strained attention, looking for a guilty smile. But either he did not know how to read their faces, or not one of these women felt herself to be guilty; he read on every face nothing but a blank expression of everyday vulgar boredom and complacency. Stupid faces, stupid smiles, harsh, stupid voices, insolent movements, and nothing else. Apparently each of them had in the past a romance with an accountant based on underclothes for fifty roubles, and looked for no other charm in the present but coffee, a dinner of three courses, wines, quadrilles, sleeping till two in the afternoon. . . .

Finding no guilty smile, Vassilyev began to look whether there was not one intelligent face. And his attention was caught by one pale, rather sleepy, exhausted-looking face. . . . It was a dark woman, not very young, wearing a dress covered with spangles; she was sitting in an easy-chair, looking at the floor lost in thought. Vassilyev walked from one corner of the room to the other, and, as though casually, sat down beside her.

"I must begin with something trivial," he thought, "and pass to what is serious. . . ."

"What a pretty dress you have!" and with his finger he touched the gold fringe of her fichu.

"Oh, is it? . . ." said the dark woman listlessly.

"What province do you come from?"

"I? From a distance. . . . From Tchernigov."

"A fine province. It's nice there."

"Any place seems nice when one is not in it."

"It's a pity I cannot describe nature," thought Vassilyev. "I might touch her by a description of nature in Tchernigov. No doubt she loves the place if she has been born there."

"Are you dull here?" he asked.

"Of course I am dull."

"Why don't you go away from here if you are dull?"

"Where should I go to? Go begging or what?"

"Begging would be easier than living here."

"How do you know that? Have you begged?"

"Yes, when I hadn't the money to study. Even if I hadn't, anyone could understand that. A beggar is anyway a free man, and you are a slave."

The dark woman stretched, and watched with sleepy eyes the footman who was bringing a trayful of glasses and seltzer water.

"Stand me a glass of porter," she said, and yawned again.

"Porter," thought Vassilyev. "And what if your brother or mother walked in at this moment? What would you say? And what would they say? There would be porter then, I imagine. . . ."

All at once there was the sound of weeping. From the adjoining room, from which the footman had brought the seltzer water, a fair man with a red face and angry eyes ran in quickly. He was followed by the tall, stout "madam," who was shouting in a shrill voice:

"Nobody has given you leave to slap girls on the cheeks! We have visitors better than you, and they don't fight! Impostor!"

A hubbub arose. Vassilyev was frightened and turned pale. In the next room there was the sound of bitter, genuine weeping, as though of someone insulted. And he realized that there were real people living here who, like people everywhere else, felt insulted, suffered, wept, and cried for help. The feeling of oppressive hate and disgust gave way to an acute feeling of pity and anger against the aggressor. He rushed into the room where there was weeping. Across rows of bottles on a marble-top table he distinguished a suffering face, wet with tears, stretched out his hands towards that face, took a step towards the table, but at once drew back in horror. The weeping girl was drunk.

As he made his way through the noisy crowd gathered about the fair man, his heart sank and he felt frightened like a child; and it seemed to him

that in this alien, incomprehensible world people
wanted to pursue him, to beat him, to pelt him
with filthy words. . . . He tore down his coat
from the hatstand and ran headlong downstairs.

V.

Leaning against the fence, he stood near the
house waiting for his friends to come out. The
sounds of the pianos and violins, gay, reckless,
insolent, and mournful, mingled in the air in a
sort of chaos, and this tangle of sounds seemed
again like an unseen orchestra tuning up on the
roofs. If one looked upwards into the darkness,
the black background was all spangled with white,
moving spots: it was snow falling. As the snowflakes came into the light they floated round
lazily in the air like down, and still more lazily
fell to the ground. The snowflakes whirled
thickly round Vassilyev and hung upon his beard,
his eyelashes, his eyebrows. . . . The cabmen,
the horses, and the passers-by were white.

"And how can the snow fall in this street!"
thought Vassilyev. "Damnation take these
houses!"

His legs seemed to be giving way from fatigue,
simply from having run down the stairs; he gasped
for breath as though he had been climbing uphill,
his heart beat so loudly that he could hear it.
He was consumed by a desire to get out of the
street as quickly as possible and to go home, but
even stronger was his desire to wait for his companions and vent upon them his oppressive feeling.

There was much he did not understand in these houses, the souls of ruined women were a mystery to him as before; but it was clear to him that the thing was far worse than could have been believed. If that sinful woman who had poisoned herself was called fallen, it was difficult to find a fitting name for all these who were dancing now to this tangle of sound and uttering long, loathsome sentences.   They were not on the road to ruin, but ruined.

"There is vice," he thought, "but neither consciousness of sin nor hope of salvation.   They are sold and bought, steeped in wine and abominations, while they, like sheep, are stupid, indifferent, and don't understand.   My God!   My God!"

It was clear to him, too, that everything that is called human dignity, personal rights, the Divine image and semblance, were defiled to their very foundations—" to the very marrow," as drunkards say—and that not only the street and the stupid women were responsible for it.

A group of students, white with snow, passed him, laughing and talking gaily; one, a tall thin fellow, stopped, glanced into Vassilyev's face, and said in a drunken voice:

"One of us!   A bit on, old man?   Aha-ha! Never mind, have a good time!   Don't be downhearted, old chap!"

He took Vassilyev by the shoulder and pressed his cold wet moustache against his cheek, then he slipped, staggered, and, waving both hands, cried:

"Hold on!   Don't upset!"

And laughing, he ran to overtake his companions.

Through the noise came the sound of the artist's voice:

"Don't you dare to hit the women! I won't let you, damnation take you! You scoundrels!"

The medical student appeared in the doorway. He looked from side to side, and seeing Vassilyev, said in an agitated voice:

"You here! I tell you it's really impossible to go anywhere with Yegor! What a fellow he is! I don't understand him! He has got up a scene! Do you hear? Yegor!" he shouted at the door. "Yegor!"

"I won't allow you to hit women!" the artist's piercing voice sounded from above. Something heavy and lumbering rolled down the stairs. It was the artist falling headlong. Evidently he had been pushed downstairs.

He picked himself up from the ground, shook his hat, and, with an angry and indignant face, brandished his fist towards the top of the stairs and shouted:

"Scoundrels! Torturers! Bloodsuckers! I won't allow you to hit them! To hit a weak, drunken woman! Oh, you brutes! . . ."

"Yegor! . . . Come, Yegor! . . ." the medical student began imploring him. "I give you my word of honour I'll never come with you again. On my word of honour I won't!"

Little by little the artist was pacified and the friends went homewards.

"Against my will an unknown force," hummed the medical student, "has led me to these mournful shores."

"Behold the mill," the artist chimed in a little later, "in ruins now. What a lot of snow, Holy Mother! Grisha, why did you go? You are a funk, a regular old woman."

Vassilyev walked behind his companions, looked at their backs, and thought:

"One of two things: either we only fancy prostitution is an evil, and we exaggerate it; or, if prostitution really is as great an evil as is generally assumed, these dear friends of mine are as much slave-owners, violators, and murderers, as the inhabitants of Syria and Cairo, that are described in the 'Neva.' Now they are singing, laughing, talking sense, but haven't they just been exploiting hunger, ignorance, and stupidity? They have—I have been a witness of it. What is the use of their humanity, their medicine, their painting? The science, art, and lofty sentiments of these soul-destroyers remind me of the piece of bacon in the story. Two brigands murdered a beggar in a forest; they began sharing his clothes between them, and found in his wallet a piece of bacon. 'Well found,' said one of them; 'let us have a bit.' 'What do you mean? How can you?' cried the other in horror. 'Have you forgotten that to-day is Wednesday?' And they would not eat it. After murdering a man, they came out of the forest in the firm conviction that they were keeping the fast. In the same way these men, after buying women, go their way imagining that they are artists and men of science. . . ."

"Listen!" he said sharply and angrily. "Why do you come here? Is it possible—is it possible you don't understand how horrible it is? Your medical books tell you that every one of these women dies prematurely of consumption or something; art tells you that morally they are dead even earlier. Every one of them dies because she has in her time to entertain five hundred men on an average, let us say. Each one of them is killed by five hundred men. You are among those five hundred! If each of you in the course of your lives visits this place or others like it two hundred and fifty times, it follows that one woman is killed for every two of you! Can't you understand that? Isn't it horrible to murder, two of you, three of you, five of you, a foolish, hungry woman! Ah! isn't it awful, my God!"

"I knew it would end like that," the artist said, frowning. "We ought not to have gone with this fool and ass! You imagine you have grand notions in your head now, ideas, don't you? No, it's the devil knows what, but not ideas. You are looking at me now with hatred and repulsion, but I tell you it's better you should set up twenty more houses like those than look like that. There's more vice in your expression than in the whole street! Come along, Volodya, let him go to the devil! He's a fool and an ass, and that's all. . . ."

"We human beings do murder each other," said the medical student. "It's immoral, of course, but philosophizing doesn't help it. Good-bye!"

At Trubnoy Square the friends said good-bye and parted. When he was left alone, Vassilyev strode rapidly along the boulevard. He felt frightened of the darkness, of the snow which was falling in heavy flakes on the ground, and seemed as though it would cover up the whole world; he felt frightened of the street lamps shining with pale light through the clouds of snow. His soul was possessed by an unaccountable, faint-hearted terror. Passers-by came towards him from time to time, but he timidly moved to one side; it seemed to him that women, none but women, were coming from all sides and staring at him. . . .

"It's beginning," he thought: "I am going to have a breakdown."

VI.

At home he lay on his bed and said, shuddering all over: "They are alive! Alive! My God, those women are alive!"

He encouraged his imagination in all sorts of ways to picture himself the brother of a fallen woman, or her father; then a fallen woman herself, with her painted cheeks; and it all moved him to horror.

It seemed to him that he must settle the question at once at all costs, and that this question was not one that did not concern him, but was his own personal problem. He made an immense effort, repressed his despair, and, sitting on the bed, holding his head in his hands, began thinking how one could save all the women he had seen that day. The method for attacking problems of all kinds was, as he was an educated man, well known to him. And however excited he was, he strictly adhered to that method. He recalled the history of the problem and its literature, and for a quarter of an hour he paced from one end of the room to the other trying to remember all the methods practised at the present time for saving women. He had very many good friends and acquaintances who lived in lodgings in Petersburg. . . . Among them were a good many honest and self-sacrificing men. Some of them had attempted to save women. . . .

"All these not very numerous attempts," thought Vassilyev, "can be divided into three groups. Some, after buying the woman out of the brothel, took a room for her, bought her a sewing-machine, and she became a sempstress. And whether he wanted to or not, after having bought her out he made her his mistress; then when he had taken his degree, he went away and handed her into the keeping of some other decent man as though she were a thing. And the fallen woman remained a fallen woman. Others, after buying her out, took a lodging apart for her, bought the inevitable sewing-machine, and tried teaching her to read, preaching at her and giving her books. The woman lived and sewed as long as it was interesting and a novelty to her, then getting bored, began receiving men on the sly, or ran away and went back where she could sleep till three o'clock, drink coffee, and have good dinners. The third class, the most ardent and self-sacrificing, had taken a bold, resolute step. They had married them. And when the insolent and spoilt, or stupid and crushed animal became

a wife, the head of a household, and afterwards
a mother, it turned her whole existence and attitude
to life upside down, so that it was hard to recognize
the fallen woman afterwards in the wife and the
mother. Yes, marriage was the best and perhaps
the only means."

" But it is impossible!" Vassilyev said aloud,
and he sank upon his bed. " I, to begin with,
could not marry one ! To do that one must be
a saint and be unable to feel hatred or repulsion.
But supposing that I, the medical student, and the
artist, mastered ourselves and did marry them—
suppose they were all married. What would be
the result ? The result would be that while
here in Moscow they were being married, some
Smolensk accountant would be debauching
another lot, and that lot would be streaming
here to fill the vacant places, together with others
from Saratov, Nizhni-Novgorod, Warsaw. . . .
And what is one to do with the hundred thousand in London ? What's one to do with those
in Hamburg ?"

The lamp in which the oil had burnt down began
to smoke. Vassilyev did not notice it. He began
pacing to and fro again, still thinking. Now he
put the question differently: what must be done
that fallen women should not be needed ? For
that, it was essential that the men who buy
them and do them to death should feel all
the immorality of their share in enslaving them
and should be horrified. One must save the
men.

" One won't do anything by art and science, that

is clear . . ." thought Vassilyev. "The only
way out of it is missionary work."

And he began to dream how he would the next
evening stand at the corner of the street and say
to every passer-by: "Where are you going and
what for? Have some fear of God!"

He would turn to the apathetic cabmen and say
to them: "Why are you staying here? Why
aren't you revolted? Why aren't you indignant?
I suppose you believe in God and know that it is a
sin, that people go to hell for it? Why don't you
speak? It is true that they are strangers to you,
but you know even they have fathers, brothers
like yourselves. . . ."

One of Vassilyev's friends had once said of him
that he was a talented man. There are all sorts
of talents—talent for writing, talent for the stage,
talent for art; but he had a peculiar talent—a
talent for *humanity*. He possessed an extraordinarily fine delicate scent for pain in general.
As a good actor reflects in himself the movements
and voice of others, so Vassilyev could reflect in
his soul the sufferings of others. When he saw
tears, he wept; beside a sick man, he felt sick
himself and moaned; if he saw an act of violence,
he felt as though he himself were the victim of it,
he was frightened as a child, and in his fright ran
to help. The pain of others worked on his nerves,
excited him, roused him to a state of frenzy, and
soon.

Whether this friend were right I don't know,
but what Vassilyev experienced when he thought
this question was settled was something like inspi-

ration. He cried and laughed, spoke aloud the
words that he should say next day, felt a fervent
love for those who would listen to him and would
stand beside him at the corner of the street to
preach; he sat down to write letters, made vows
to himself. . . .

All this was like inspiration also from the fact
that it did not last long. Vassilyev was soon
tired. The cases in London, in Hamburg, in
Warsaw, weighed upon him by their mass as a
mountain weighs upon the earth; he felt dis-
pirited, bewildered, in the face of this mass; he
remembered that he had not a gift for words, that
he was cowardly and timid, that indifferent people
would not be willing to listen and understand him,
a law student in his third year, a timid and insignificant person; that genuine missionary work
included not only teaching but deeds. . . .

When it was daylight and carriages were already
beginning to rumble in the street, Vassilyev was
lying motionless on the sofa, staring into space.
He was no longer thinking of the women, nor of
the men, nor of missionary work. His whole
attention was turned upon the spiritual agony
which was torturing him. It was a dull, vague,
undefined anguish akin to misery, to an extreme
form of terror, and to despair. He could point
to the place where the pain was, in his breast under
his heart; but he could not compare it with anything. In the past he had had acute toothache,
he had had pleurisy and neuralgia, but all that
was insignificant compared with this spiritual
anguish. In the presence of that pain life seemed

loathsome. The dissertation, the excellent work he had written already, the people he loved, the salvation of fallen women—everything that only the day before he had cared about or been indifferent to, now when he thought of them irritated him in the same way as the noise of the carriages, the scurrying footsteps of the waiters in the passage, the daylight. . . . If at that moment someone had performed a great deed of mercy or had committed a revolting outrage, he would have felt the same repulsion for both actions. Of all the thoughts that strayed through his mind only two did not irritate him: one was that at every moment he had the power to kill himself, the other that this agony would not last more than three days. This last he knew by experience.

After lying for a while he got up and, wringing his hands, walked about the room, not as usual from corner to corner, but round the room beside the walls. As he passed he glanced at himself in the looking-glass. His face looked pale and sunken, his temples looked hollow, his eyes were bigger, darker, more staring, as though they belonged to someone else, and they had an expression of insufferable mental agony.

At midday the artist knocked at the door.

" Grigory, are you at home ?" he asked.

Getting no answer, he stood for a minute, pondered, and answered himself in Little Russian: " Nay. The confounded fellow has gone to the University."

And he went away. Vassilyev lay down on the bed, and, thrusting his head under the pillow,

began crying with agony, and the more freely
his tears flowed the more terrible his mental
anguish became. As it began to get dark, he
thought of the agonizing night awaiting him, and
was overcome by a horrible despair. He dressed
quickly, ran out of his room, and, leaving his door
wide open, for no object or reason went out into
the street. Without asking himself where he
should go, he walked quickly along Sadovoy
Street.

Snow was falling as heavily as the day before;
it was thawing. Thrusting his hands into his
sleeves, shuddering and frightened at the noises,
at the tram-bells, and at the passers-by, Vassilyev
walked along Sadovoy Street as far as Suharev
Tower; then to the Red Gate; from there he turned
off to Basmannya Street. He went into a tavern
and drank off a big glass of vodka, but that did
not make him feel better. When he reached
Razgulya he turned to the right, and strode along
side streets in which he had never been before in
his life. He reached the old bridge by which the
Yauza runs gurgling, and from which one can see
long rows of lights in the windows of the Red
Barracks. To distract his spiritual anguish by
some new sensation or some other pain, Vassilyev,
not knowing what to do, crying and shuddering,
undid his greatcoat and jacket and exposed his
bare chest to the wet snow and the wind. But
that did not lessen his suffering either. Then he
bent down over the rail of the bridge and looked
down into the black, yeasty Yauza, and he longed
to plunge down head-foremost; not from loathing

for life, not for the sake of suicide, but in order to bruise himself at least, and by one pain to ease the other. But the black water, the darkness, the deserted banks covered with snow were terrifying. He shivered and walked on. He walked up and down by the Red Barracks, then turned back and went down to a copse, from the copse back to the bridge again.

"No, home, home!" he thought. "At home I believe it's better. . . ."

And he went back. When he reached home he pulled off his wet coat and cap, began pacing round the room, and went on pacing round and round without stopping till morning.

VII.

When next morning the artist and the medical student went in to him, he was moving about the room with his shirt torn, biting his hands and moaning with pain.

"For God's sake!" he sobbed when he saw his friends, "take me where you please, do what you can; but for God's sake, save me quickly! I shall kill myself!"

The artist turned pale and was helpless. The medical student, too, almost shed tears, but considering that doctors ought to be cool and composed in every emergency, said coldly:

"It's a nervous breakdown. But it's nothing. Let us go at once to the doctor."

"Wherever you like, only for God's sake, make haste!"

IX.

4

" Don't excite yourself. You must try and control yourself."

The artist and the medical student with trembling hands put Vassilyev's coat and hat on and led him out into the street.

" Mihail Sergeyitch has been wanting to make your acquaintance for a long time," the medical student said on the way. " He is a very nice man and thoroughly good at his work. He took his degree in 1882, and he has an immense practice already. He treats students as though he were one himself."

" Make haste, make haste ! . . ." Vassilyev urged.

Mihail Sergeyitch, a stout, fair-haired doctor, received the friends with politeness and frigid dignity, and smiled only on one side of his face.

" Rybnikov and Mayer have spoken to me of your illness already," he said. " Very glad to be of service to you. Well ? Sit down, I beg. . . ."

He made Vassilyev sit down in a big armchair near the table, and moved a box of cigarettes towards him.

" Now then !" he began, stroking his knees. " Let us get to work. . . . How old are you ?"

He asked questions and the medical student answered them. He asked whether Vassilyev's father had suffered from certain special diseases, whether he drank to excess, whether he were remarkable for cruelty or any peculiarities. He made similar enquiries about his grandfather, mother, sisters, and brothers. On learning that his mother had a beautiful voice and sometimes acted on the stage, he grew more animated at once, and asked:

" Excuse me, but don't you remember, perhaps, your mother had a passion for the stage?"

Twenty minutes passed. Vassilyev was annoyed by the way the doctor kept stroking his knees and talking of the same thing.

" So far as I understand your questions, doctor," he said, " you want to know whether my illness is hereditary or not. It is not."

The doctor proceeded to ask Vassilyev whether he had had any secret vices as a boy, or had received injuries to his head; whether he had had any aberrations, any peculiarities, or exceptional propensities. Half the questions usually asked by doctors of their patients can be left unanswered without the slightest ill effect on the health, but Mihail Sergeyitch, the medical student, and the artist all looked as though if Vassilyev failed to answer one question all would be lost. As he received answers, the doctor for some reason noted them down on a slip of paper. On learning that Vassilyev had taken his degree in natural science, and was now studying law, the doctor pondered.

" He wrote a first-rate piece of original work last year, . . ." said the medical student.

" I beg your pardon, but don't interrupt me; you prevent me from concentrating," said the doctor, and he smiled on one side of his face. " Though, of course, that does enter into the diagnosis. Intense intellectual work, nervous exhaustion. . . . Yes, yes. . . . And do you drink vodka?" he said, addressing Vassilyev.

" Very rarely."

Another twenty minutes passed. The medical student began telling the doctor in a low voice his opinion as to the immediate cause of the attack, and described how the day before yesterday the artist, Vassilyev, and he had visited S. Street.

The indifferent, reserved, and frigid tone in which his friends and the doctor spoke of the women and that miserable street struck Vassilyev as strange in the extreme. . . .

" Doctor, tell me one thing only," he said, controlling himself so as not to speak rudely. " Is prostitution an evil or not ?"

" My dear fellow, who disputes it ?" said the doctor, with an expression that suggested that he had settled all such questions for himself long ago. " Who disputes it ?"

" You are a mental doctor, aren't you ?" Vassilyev asked curtly.

" Yes, a mental doctor."

" Perhaps all of you are right !" said Vassilyev, getting up and beginning to walk from one end of the room to the other. " Perhaps ! But it all seems marvellous to me ! That I should have taken my degree in two faculties you look upon as a great achievement; because I have written a work which in three years will be thrown aside and forgotten, I am praised up to the skies; but because I cannot speak of fallen women as unconcernedly as of these chairs, I am being examined by a doctor, I am called mad, I am pitied !"

Vassilyev for some reason felt all at once un-

utterably sorry for himself, and his companions,
and all the people he had seen two days before,
and for the doctor; he burst into tears and sank
into a chair.

His friends looked enquiringly at the doctor.
The latter, with the air of completely comprehend-
ing the tears and the despair, of feeling himself a
specialist in that line, went up to Vassilyev and,
without a word, gave him some medicine to drink;
and then, when he was calmer, undressed him and
began to investigate the degree of sensibility of
the skin, the reflex action of the knees, and so on.

And Vassilyev felt easier. When he came out
from the doctor's he was beginning to feel ashamed;
the rattle of the carriages no longer irritated him,
and the load at his heart grew lighter and lighter
as though it were melting away. He had two
prescriptions in his hand: one was for bromide,
one was for morphia. . . . He had taken all
these remedies before!

In the street he stood still and, saying good-bye
to his friends, dragged himself languidly to the
University.

MISERY

MISERY

"To whom shall I tell my grief?"

THE twilight of evening. Big flakes of wet snow
are whirling lazily about the street-lamps, which
have just been lighted, and lying in a thin soft
layer on roofs, horses' backs, shoulders, caps. Iona
Potapov, the sledge-driver, is all white like a ghost.
He sits on the box without stirring, bent as double
as the living body can be bent. If a regular snowdrift fell on him it seems as though even then he
would not think it necessary to shake it off.
. . . His little mare is white and motionless too.
Her stillness, the angularity of her lines, and the
stick-like straightness of her legs, make her look
like a halfpenny gingerbread horse. She is probably
lost in thought. Anyone who has been torn
away from the plough, from the familiar grey
landscapes, and cast into this slough, full of
monstrous lights, of unceasing uproar and hurrying people, is bound to think.

It is a long time since Iona and his nag have
budged. They came out of the yard before dinner-
time, and not a single fare yet. But now the
shades of evening are falling on the town. The
pale light of the street-lamps changes to a vivid
colour, and the bustle of the street grows noisier.

57

"Sledge to Vyborgskaya!" Iona hears. "Sledge!"

Iona starts, and through his snow-plastered eyelashes sees an officer in a military overcoat with a hood over his head.

"To Vyborgskaya," repeats the officer. "Are you asleep? To Vyborgskaya!"

In token of assent Iona gives a tug at the reins which sends cakes of snow flying from the horse's back and shoulders. The officer gets into the sledge. The sledge-driver clicks to the horse, cranes his neck like a swan, rises in his seat, and more from habit than necessity brandishes his whip. The mare cranes her neck, too, crooks her stick-like legs, and hesitatingly sets off. . . .

"Where are you shoving, you devil?" Iona immediately hears shouts from the dark mass shifting to and fro before him. "Where the devil are you going? Keep to the r-right!"

"You don't know how to drive! Keep to the right," says the officer angrily.

A coachman driving a carriage swears at him; a pedestrian crossing the road and brushing the horse's nose with his shoulder looks at him angrily and shakes the snow off his sleeve. Iona fidgets on the box as though he were sitting on thorns, jerks his elbows, and turns his eyes about like one possessed, as though he did not know where he was or why he was there.

"What rascals they all are!" says the officer jocosely. "They are simply doing their best to run up against you or fall under the horse's feet. They must be doing it on purpose."

Iona looks at his fare and moves his lips. . . .
Apparently he means to say something, but
nothing comes but a sniff.

" What ?" enquires the officer.

Iona gives a wry smile, and straining his throat,
brings out huskily: " My son . . . er . . . my son
died this week, sir."

" H'm ! What did he die of ?"

Iona turns his whole body round to his fare, and
says:

" Who can tell ! It must have been from
fever. . . . He lay three days in the hospital
and then he died. . . . God's will."

" Turn round, you devil !" comes out of the
darkness. " Have you gone cracked, you old dog ?
Look where you are going !"

" Drive on ! drive on ! . . ." says the officer.
" We shan't get there till to-morrow going on
like this. Hurry up !"

The sledge-driver cranes his neck again, rises
in his seat, and with heavy grace swings his whip.
Several times he looks round at the officer, but the
latter keeps his eyes shut and is apparently disin-
clined to listen. Putting his fare down at Vyborgskaya, Iona stops by a restaurant, and again sits
huddled up on the box. . . . Again the wet snow
paints him and his horse white. One hour passes,
and then another. . . .

Three young men, two tall and thin, one short
and hunchbacked, come up, railing at each other
and loudly stamping on the pavement with their
goloshes.

" Cabby, to the Police Bridge !" the hunchback

cries in a cracked voice. " The three of us, . . .
twenty kopecks !"

Iona tugs at the reins and clicks to his horse.
Twenty kopecks is not a fair price, but he has no
thoughts for that. Whether it is a rouble or
whether it is five kopecks does not matter to him
now so long as he has a fare. . . . The three
young men, shoving each other and using bad
language, go up to the sledge, and all three try to
sit down at once. The question remains to be
settled : Which are to sit down and which one is to
stand ? After a long altercation, ill-temper, and
abuse, they come to the conclusion that the hunchback must stand because he is the shortest.

" Well, drive on," says the hunchback in his
cracked voice, settling himself and breathing down
Iona's neck. " Cut along ! What a cap you've
got, my friend ! You wouldn't find a worse one
in all Petersburg. . . ."

" He—he ! . . . he—he ! . . ." laughs Iona.
" It's nothing to boast of !"

" Well, then, nothing to boast of, drive on !
Are you going to drive like this all the way ? Eh ?
Shall I give you one in the neck ?"

" My head aches," says one of the tall ones.
" At the Dukmasovs' yesterday Vaska and I
drank four bottles of brandy between us."

" I can't make out why you talk such stuff,"
says the other tall one angrily. " You lie like a
brute."

" Strike me dead, it's the truth ! . . ."

" It's about as true as that a louse coughs."

" He-he !" grins Iona. " Me-er-ry gentlemen !"

"Tfoo! the devil take you!" cries the hunchback indignantly. "Will you get on, you old plague, or won't you? Is that the way to drive? Give her one with the whip. Hang it all! give it her well."

Iona feels behind his back the jolting person and quivering voice of the hunchback. He hears abuse addressed to him, he sees people, and the feeling of loneliness begins little by little to be less heavy on his heart. The hunchback swears at him, till he chokes over some elaborately whimsical string of epithets and is overpowered by his cough. His tall companions begin talking of a certain Nadyezhda Petrovna. Iona looks round at them. Waiting till there is a brief pause, he looks round once more and says:

"This week . . . er . . . my . . . er . . . son died!"

"We shall all die, . . ." says the hunchback with a sigh, wiping his lips after coughing. "Come, drive on! drive on! My friends, I simply cannot stand crawling like this! When will he get us there?"

"Well, you give him a little encouragement . . . one in the neck!"

"Do you hear, you old plague? I'll make you smart. If one stands on ceremony with fellows like you one may as well walk. Do you hear, you old dragon? Or don't you care a hang what we say?"

And Iona hears rather than feels a slap on the back of his neck.

"He-he! . . ." he laughs. "Merry gentlemen. . . . God give you health!"

" Cabman, are you married ?" asks one of the tall ones.

" I ? He-he ! Me-er-ry gentlemen. The only wife for me now is the damp earth. . . . He-ho-ho ! . . . The grave that is ! . . . Here my son's dead and I am alive. . . . It's a strange thing, death has come in at the wrong door. . . . Instead of coming for me it went for my son. . . ."

And Iona turns round to tell them how his son died, but at that point the hunchback gives a faint sigh and announces that, thank God ! they have arrived at last. After taking his twenty kopecks, Iona gazes for a long while after the revellers, who disappear into a dark entry. Again he is alone and again there is silence for him. . . . The misery which has been for a brief space eased comes back again and tears his heart more cruelly than ever. With a look of anxiety and suffering Iona's eyes stray restlessly among the crowds moving to and fro on both sides of the street: can he not find among those thousands someone who will listen to him ? But the crowds flit by heedless of him and his misery. . . . His misery is immense, beyond all bounds. If Iona's heart were to burst and his misery to flow out, it would flood the whole world, it seems, but yet it is not seen. It has found a hiding-place in such an insignificant shell that one would not have found it with a candle by daylight. . . .

Iona sees a house-porter with a parcel and makes up his mind to address him.

" What time will it be, friend ?" he asks.

" Going on for ten. . . . Why have you stopped here ? Drive on !"

Iona drives a few paces away, bends himself double, and gives himself up to his misery. He feels it is no good to appeal to people. But before five minutes have passed he draws himself up, shakes his head as though he feels a sharp pain, and tugs at the reins. . . . He can bear it no longer.

" Back to the yard !" he thinks. " To the yard !"

And his little mare, as though she knew his thoughts, falls to trotting. An hour and a half later Iona is sitting by a big dirty stove. On the stove, on the floor, and on the benches are people snoring. The air is full of smells and stuffiness. Iona looks at the sleeping figures, scratches himself, and regrets that he has come home so early. . . .

" I have not earned enough to pay for the oats, even," he thinks. " That's why I am so miserable. A man who knows how to do his work, . . . who has had enough to eat, and whose horse has had enough to eat, is always at ease. . . ."

In one of the corners a young cabman gets up, clears his throat sleepily, and makes for the water-bucket.

" Want a drink ?" Iona asks him.

" Seems so."

" May it do you good. . . . But my son is dead, mate. . . . Do you hear ? This week in the hospital. . . . It's a queer business. . . ."

Iona looks to see the effect produced by his

words, but he sees nothing. The young man has covered his head over and is already asleep. The old man sighs and scratches himself. . . . Just as the young man had been thirsty for water, he thirsts for speech. His son will soon have been dead a week, and he has not really talked to anybody yet . . . . He wants to talk of it properly, with deliberation. . . . He wants to tell how his son was taken ill, how he suffered, what he said before he died, how he died. . . . He wants to describe the funeral, and how he went to the hospital to get his son's clothes. He still has his daughter Anisya in the country. . . . And he wants to talk about her too. . . . Yes, he has plenty to talk about now. His listener ought to sigh and exclaim and lament. . . . It would be even better to talk to women. Though they are silly creatures, they blubber at the first word.

" Let's go out and have a look at the mare," Iona thinks. " There is always time for sleep. . . . You'll have sleep enough, no fear. . . ."

He puts on his coat and goes into the stables where his mare is standing. He thinks about oats, about hay, about the weather. . . . He cannot think about his son when he is alone. . . . To talk about him with someone is possible, but to think of him and picture him is insufferable anguish. . . .

" Are you munching?" Iona asks his mare, seeing her shining eyes. " There, munch away, munch away. . . . Since we have not earned enough for oats, we will eat hay. . . . Yes, . . . I have grown too old to drive. . . . My son ought

to be driving, not I. . . . He was a real cabman.
. . . He ought to have lived. . . ."

Iona is silent for a while, and then he goes on:

"That's how it is, old girl. . . . Kuzma
Ionitch is gone. . . . He said good-bye to me.
. . . He went and died for no reason. . . . Now,
suppose you had a little colt, and you were own
mother to that little colt. . . . And all at once
that same little colt went and died. . . . You'd
be sorry, wouldn't you ? . . ."

The little mare munches, listens, and breathes
on her master's hands. Iona is carried away and
tells her all about it.

to be driving and I..... He was a real coachman
..... He ought to have lived.....

Iona is silent for a while, and then he goes on:
"That's how it is, old girl..... Kuzma
Ionitch is gone..... He said good-bye to me.....
He went and died for no reason..... Now
suppose you had a little colt, and you were own
mother to that little colt..... And all at once
that same little colt went and died..... You'd
be sorry, wouldn't you?....."

The little mare munches, listens, and breathes
on her master's hands. Iona is carried away and
tells her all about it.

CHAMPAGNE

A WAYFARER'S STORY

CHAMPAGNE

A WAYFARER'S STORY

IN the year in which my story begins I had a job
at a little station on one of our south-western
railways. Whether I had a gay or a dull life
at the station you can judge from the fact that
for fifteen miles round there was not one human
habitation, not one woman, not one decent tavern;
and in those days I was young, strong, hot-
headed, giddy, and foolish. The only distraction
I could possibly find was in the windows of the
passenger trains, and in the vile vodka which the
Jews drugged with thorn-apple. Sometimes there
would be a glimpse of a woman's head at a carriage
window, and one would stand like a statue without
breathing and stare at it until the train turned
into an almost invisible speck; or one would drink
all one could of the loathsome vodka till one was
stupefied and did not feel the passing of the long
hours and days. Upon me, a native of the north,
the steppe produced the effect of a deserted Tatar
cemetery. In the summer the steppe with its
solemn calm, the monotonous chur of the grasshoppers, the transparent moonlight from which
one could not hide, reduced me to listless melancholy; and in the winter the irreproachable white

ness of the steppe, its cold distance, long nights and howling wolves oppressed me like a heavy nightmare. There were several people living at the station: my wife and I, a deaf and scrofulous telegraph clerk, and three watchmen. My assistant, a young man who was in consumption, used to go for treatment to the town, where he stayed for months at a time, leaving his duties to me together with the right of pocketing his salary. I had no children, no cake would have tempted visitors to come and see me, and I could only visit other officials on the line, and that no oftener than once a month.

I remember my wife and I saw the New Year in. We sat at table, chewed lazily, and heard the deaf telegraph clerk monotonously tapping on his apparatus in the next room. I had already drunk five glasses of drugged vodka, and, propping my heavy head on my fist, thought of my overpowering boredom from which there was no escape, while my wife sat beside me and did not take her eyes off me. She looked at me as no one can look but a woman who has nothing in this world but a handsome husband. She loved me madly, slavishly, and not merely my good looks, or my soul, but my sins, my ill-humour and boredom, and even my cruelty when, in drunken fury, not knowing how to vent my ill-humour, I tormented her with reproaches.

In spite of the boredom which was consuming me, we were preparing to see the New Year in with exceptional festiveness, and were awaiting midnight with some impatience. The fact is, we had in reserve two bottles of champagne, the real thing, with the label of Veuve Clicquot; this treasure I had won the previous autumn in a bet with the station-master of D. when I was drinking with him at a christening. It sometimes happens during a lesson in mathematics, when the very air is still with boredom, a butterfly flutters into the class-room; the boys toss their heads and begin watching its flight with interest, as though they saw before them not a butterfly but something new and strange; in the same way ordinary champagne, chancing to come into our dreary station, roused us. We sat in silence looking alternately at the clock and at the bottles.

When the hands pointed to five minutes to twelve I slowly began uncorking a bottle. I don't know whether I was affected by the vodka, or whether the bottle was wet, but all I remember is that when the cork flew up to the ceiling with a bang, my bottle slipped out of my hands and fell on the floor. Not more than a glass of the wine was spilt, as I managed to catch the bottle and put my thumb over the foaming neck.

" Well, may the New Year bring you happiness!" I said, filling two glasses. "Drink!"

My wife took her glass and fixed her frightened eyes on me. Her face was pale and wore a look of horror.

" Did you drop the bottle?" she asked.

" Yes. But what of that?"

" It's unlucky," she said, putting down her glass and turning paler still. "It's a bad omen. It means that some misfortune will happen to us this year."

"What a silly thing you are," I sighed. "You are a clever woman, and yet you talk as much nonsense as an old nurse. Drink."

"God grant it is nonsense, but . . . something is sure to happen ! You'll see."

She did not even sip her glass, she moved away and sank into thought. I uttered a few stale commonplaces about superstition, drank half a bottle, paced up and down, and then went out of the room.

Outside there was the still frosty night in all its cold, inhospitable beauty. The moon and two white fluffy clouds beside it hung just over the station, motionless as though glued to the spot, and looked as though waiting for something. A faint transparent light came from them and touched the white earth softly, as though afraid of wounding her modesty, and lighted up everything—the snowdrifts, the embankment. . . . It was still.

I walked along the railway embankment.

"Silly woman," I thought, looking at the sky spangled with brilliant stars. "Even if one admits that omens sometimes tell the truth, what evil can happen to us ? The misfortunes we have endured already, and which are facing us now, are so great that it is difficult to imagine anything worse. What further harm can you do a fish which has been caught and fried and served up with sauce ?"

A poplar covered with hoar-frost looked in the

bluish darkness like a giant wrapt in a shroud. It looked at me sullenly and dejectedly, as though like me it realized its loneliness. I stood a long while looking at it.

" My youth is thrown away for nothing, like a useless cigarette end," I went on musing. " My parents died when I was a little child, I was expelled from the high school, I was born of a noble family, but I have received neither education nor breeding, and I have no more knowledge than the humblest mechanic. I have no refuge, no relations, no friends, no work I like. I am not fitted for anything, and in the prime of my powers I am good for nothing but to be stuffed into this little station; I have known nothing but trouble and failure all my life. What can happen worse ? "

Red lights came into sight in the distance. A train was moving towards me. The slumbering steppe listened to the sound of it. My thoughts were so bitter that it seemed to me that I was thinking aloud, and that the moan of the tele- graph wire and the rumble of the train were ex- pressing my thoughts.

" What can happen worse ? The loss of my wife ? " I wondered. " Even that is not terrible. It's no good hiding it from my conscience: I don't love my wife. I married her when I was only a wretched boy; now I am young and vigorous, and she has gone off and grown older and sillier, stuffed from her head to her heels with conventional ideas. What charm is there in her maudlin love, in her hollow chest, in her lustreless eyes ? I put up with her, but I don't love her. What can happen ?   My youth is being wasted, as the saying is, for a pinch of snuff.   Women flit before my eyes only in the carriage windows, like falling stars.   Love I never had and have not.   My manhood, my courage, my power of feeling are going to ruin. . . .   Everything is being thrown away like dirt, and all my wealth here in the steppe is not worth a farthing."

The train rushed past me with a roar and indifferently cast the glow of its red lights upon me. I saw it stop by the green lights of the station, stop for a minute and rumble off again.   After walking a mile and a half I went back.   Melancholy thoughts haunted me still.   Painful as it was to me, yet I remember I tried as it were to make my thoughts still gloomier and more melancholy.   You know people who are vain and not very clever have moments when the consciousness that they are miserable affords them positive satisfaction, and they even coquette with their misery for their own entertainment.   There was a great deal of truth in what I thought, but there was also a great deal that was absurd and conceited, and there was something boyishly defiant in my question: " What could happen worse ?"

" And what is there to happen ?" I asked myself.   " I think I have endured everything. I've been ill, I've lost money, I get reprimanded by my superiors every day, and I go hungry, and a mad wolf has run into the station yard. What more is there ?   I have been insulted, humiliated, . . . and I have insulted others in my time.   I have not been a criminal, it is true,

but I don't think I am capable of crime—I am not
afraid of being hauled up for it."

The two little clouds had moved away from the
moon and stood at a little distance, looking as
though they were whispering about something
which the moon must not know. A light breeze
was racing across the steppe, bringing the faint
rumble of the retreating train.

My wife met me at the doorway. Her eyes were
laughing gaily and her whole face was beaming
with good-humour.

"There is news for you!" she whispered.
"Make haste, go to your room and put on your
new coat: we have a visitor."

"What visitor?"

"Aunt Natalya Petrovna has just come by the
train."

"What Natalya Petrovna?"

"The wife of my uncle Semyon Fyodoritch.
You don't know her. She is a very nice, good
woman."

Probably I frowned, for my wife looked grave
and whispered rapidly:

"Of course it is queer her having come, but
don't be cross, Nikolay, and don't be hard on her.
She is unhappy, you know; Uncle Semyon Fyodoritch really is ill-natured and tyrannical, it is
difficult to live with him. She says she will only
stay three days with us, only till she gets a letter
from her brother."

My wife whispered a great deal more nonsense
to me about her despotic uncle; about the weakness of mankind in general and of young wives in

particular; about its being our duty to give shelter to all, even great sinners, and so on. Unable to make head or tail of it, I put on my new coat and went to make acquaintance with my " aunt."

A little woman with large black eyes was sitting at the table. My table, the grey walls, my roughly-made sofa, everything to the tiniest grain of dust seemed to have grown younger and more cheerful in the presence of this new, young, beautiful, and dissolute creature, who had a most subtle perfume about her. And that our visitor was a lady of easy virtue I could see from her smile, from her scent, from the peculiar way in which she glanced and made play with her eyelashes, from the tone in which she talked with my wife—a respectable woman. There was no need to tell me she had run away from her husband, that her husband was old and despotic, that she was good-natured and lively; I took it all in at the first glance. Indeed, it is doubtful whether there is a man in all Europe who cannot spot at the first glance a woman of a certain temperament.

" I did not know I had such a big nephew !" said my aunt, holding out her hand to me and smiling.

" And I did not know I had such a pretty aunt," I answered.

Supper began over again. The cork flew with a bang out of the second bottle, and my aunt swallowed half a glassful at a gulp, and when my wife went out of the room for a moment my aunt did not scruple to drain a full glass. I was drunk both with the wine and with the presence of a woman. Do you remember the song ?

> " Eyes black as pitch, eyes full of passion,
>   Eyes burning bright and beautiful,
>   How I love you,
>   How I fear you !"

I don't remember what happened next. Anyone who wants to know how love begins may read novels and long stories; I will put it shortly and in the words of the same silly song:

> " It was an evil hour
>   When first I met you."

Everything went head over heels to the devil. I remember a fearful, frantic whirlwind which sent me flying round like a feather. It lasted a long while, and swept from the face of the earth my wife and my aunt herself and my strength. From the little station in the steppe it has flung me, as you see, into this dark street.

Now tell me what further evil can happen to me?

AFTER THE THEATRE

AFTER THE THEATRE

NADYA ZELENIN had just come back with her
mamma from the theatre where she had seen a
performance of " Yevgeny Onyegin." As soon as
she reached her own room she threw off her dress,
let down her hair, and in her petticoat and white
dressing-jacket hastily sat down to the table to
write a letter like Tatyana's.

" I love you," she wrote, " but you do not love
me, do not love me !"

She wrote it and laughed.

She was only sixteen and did not yet love
anyone. She knew that an officer called Gorny
and a student called Gruzdev loved her, but now
after the opera she wanted to be doubtful of their
love. To be unloved and unhappy—how interesting that was ! There is something beautiful,
touching, and poetical about it when one loves and
the other is indifferent. Onyegin was interesting
because he was not in love at all, and Tatyana was
fascinating because she was so much in love;
but if they had been equally in love with each other
and had been happy, they would perhaps have
seemed dull.

" Leave off declaring that you love me," Nadya
went on writing, thinking of Gorny. " I cannot

believe it.   You are very clever, cultivated, serious, you have immense talent, and perhaps a brilliant future awaits you, while I am an uninteresting girl of no importance, and you know very well that I should be only a hindrance in your life.   It is true that you were attracted by me and thought you had found your ideal in me, but that was a mistake, and now you are asking yourself in despair: ' Why did I meet that girl ?'   And only your goodness of heart prevents you from owning it to yourself. . . ."

Nadya felt sorry for herself, she began to cry, and went on:

" It is hard for me to leave my mother and my brother, or I should take a nun's veil and go whither chance may lead me.   And you would be left free and would love another.   Oh, if I were dead !"

She could not make out what she had written through her tears; little rainbows were quivering on the table, on the floor, on the ceiling, as though she were looking through a prism.   She could not write, she sank back in her easy-chair and fell to thinking of Gorny.

My God ! how interesting, how fascinating men were !   Nadya recalled the fine expression, ingratiating, guilty, and soft, which came into the officer's face when one argued about music with him, and the effort he made to prevent his voice from betraying his passion.   In a society where cold haughtiness and indifference are regarded as signs of good breeding and gentlemanly bearing, one must conceal one's passions.   And he did try

to conceal them, but he did not succeed, and everyone knew very well that he had a passionate love
of music. The endless discussions about music
and the bold criticisms of people who knew nothing
about it kept him always on the strain; he was
frightened, timid, and silent. He played the piano
magnificently, like a professional pianist, and if
he had not been in the army he would certainly
have been a famous musician.

The tears on her eyes dried. Nadya remembered
that Gorny had declared his love at a Symphony
concert, and again downstairs by the hatstand
where there was a tremendous draught blowing in
all directions.

" I am very glad that you have at last made the
acquaintance of Gruzdev, our student friend,"
she went on writing. " He is a very clever man,
and you will be sure to like him. He came to see
us yesterday and stayed till two o'clock. We
were all delighted with him, and I regretted that
you had not come. He said a great deal that was
remarkable."

Nadya laid her arms on the table and leaned
her head on them, and her hair covered the letter.
She recalled that the student, too, loved her, and
that he had as much right to a letter from her as
Gorny. Wouldn't it be better after all to write to
Gruzdev? There was a stir of joy in her bosom
for no reason whatever; at first the joy was small,
and rolled in her bosom like an india-rubber ball;
then it became more massive, bigger, and rushed
like a wave. Nadya forgot Gorny and Gruzdev;
her thoughts were in a tangle and her joy grew and

grew; from her bosom it passed into her arms and legs, and it seemed as though a light, cool breeze were breathing on her head and ruffling her hair. Her shoulders quivered with subdued laughter, the table and the lamp chimney shook, too, and tears from her eyes splashed on the letter. She could not stop laughing, and to prove to herself that she was not laughing about nothing she made haste to think of something funny.

"What a funny poodle!" she said, feeling as though she would choke with laughter. "What a funny poodle!"

She thought how, after tea the evening before, Gruzdev had played with Maxim the poodle, and afterwards had told them about a very intelligent poodle who had run after a crow in the yard, and the crow had looked round at him and said: "Oh, you scamp!"

The poodle, not knowing he had to do with a learned crow, was fearfully confused and retreated in perplexity, then began barking. . . .

"No, I had better love Gruzdev," Nadya decided, and she tore up the letter to Gorny.

She fell to thinking of the student, of his love, of her love; but the thoughts in her head insisted on flowing in all directions, and she thought about everything—about her mother, about the street, about the pencil, about the piano. . . . She thought of them joyfully, and felt that everything was good, splendid, and her joy told her that this was not all, that in a little while it would be better still. Soon it would be spring, summer, going with her mother to Gorbiki. Gorny would come for his furlough, would walk about the garden with her and make love to her. Gruzdev would come too. He would play croquet and skittles with her, and would tell her wonderful things. She had a passionate longing for the garden, the darkness, the pure sky, the stars. Again her shoulders shook with laughter, and it seemed to her that there was a scent of wormwood in the room and that a twig was tapping at the window.

She went to her bed, sat down, and not knowing what to do with the immense joy which filled her with yearning, she looked at the holy image hanging at the back of her bed, and said:

"Oh, Lord God! Oh, Lord God!"

A LADY'S STORY

A LADY'S STORY

Nine years ago Pyotr Sergeyitch, the deputy prosecutor, and I were riding towards evening in
haymaking time to fetch the letters from the
station.

The weather was magnificent, but on our way
back we heard a peal of thunder, and saw an angry
black storm-cloud which was coming straight
towards us. The storm-cloud was approaching
us and we were approaching it.

Against the background of it our house and
church looked white and the tall poplars shone like
silver. There was a scent of rain and mown hay.
My companion was in high spirits. He kept
laughing and talking all sorts of nonsense. He said
it would be nice if we could suddenly come upon
a medieval castle with turreted towers, with moss
on it and owls, in which we could take shelter
from the rain and in the end be killed by a thunder-
bolt. . . .

Then the first wave raced through the rye and
a field of oats, there was a gust of wind, and the
dust flew round and round in the air. Pyotr
Sergeyitch laughed and spurred on his horse.

" It's fine !" he cried, " it's splendid !"

Infected by his gaiety, I too began laughing at

the thought that in a minute I should be drenched to the skin and might be struck by lightning.

Riding swiftly in a hurricane when one is breathless with the wind, and feels like a bird, thrills one and puts one's heart in a flutter. By the time we rode into our courtyard the wind had gone down, and big drops of rain were pattering on the grass and on the roofs. There was not a soul near the stable.

Pyotr Sergeyitch himself took the bridles off, and led the horses to their stalls. I stood in the doorway waiting for him to finish, and watching the slanting streaks of rain; the sweetish, exciting scent of hay was even stronger here than in the fields; the storm-clouds and the rain made it almost twilight.

"What a crash!" said Pyotr Sergeyitch, coming up to me after a very loud rolling peal of thunder when it seemed as though the sky were split in two. "What do you say to that?"

He stood beside me in the doorway and, still breathless from his rapid ride, looked at me. I could see that he was admiring me.

"Natalya Vladimirovna," he said, "I would give anything only to stay here a little longer and look at you. You are lovely to-day."

His eyes looked at me with delight and supplication, his face was pale. On his beard and moustache were glittering raindrops, and they, too, seemed to be looking at me with love.

"I love you," he said. "I love you, and I am happy at seeing you. I know you cannot be my wife, but I want nothing, I ask nothing; only know that I love you. Be silent, do not answer me, take no notice of it, but only know that you are dear to me and let me look at you."

His rapture affected me too; I looked at his enthusiastic face, listened to his voice which mingled with the patter of the rain, and stood as though spell-bound, unable to stir.

I longed to go on endlessly looking at his shining eyes and listening.

"You say nothing, and that is splendid," said Pyotr Sergeyitch. " Go on being silent."

I felt happy. I laughed with delight and ran through the drenching rain to the house; he laughed too, and, leaping as he went, ran after me.

Both drenched, panting, noisily clattering up the stairs like children, we dashed into the room. My father and brother, who were not used to seeing me laughing and lighthearted, looked at me in surprise and began laughing too.

The storm-clouds had passed over and the thunder had ceased, but the raindrops still glittered on Pyotr Sergeyitch's beard. The whole evening till supper-time he was singing, whistling, playing noisily with the dog and racing about the room after it, so that he nearly upset the servant with the samovar. And at supper he ate a great deal, talked nonsense, and maintained that when one eats fresh cucumbers in winter there is the fragrance of spring in one's mouth.

When I went to bed I lighted a candle and threw my window wide open, and an undefined feeling took possession of my soul. I remembered that I was free and healthy, that I had rank and

wealth, that I was beloved; above all, that I had
rank and wealth, rank and wealth, my God! how
nice that was! . . . Then, huddling up in bed
at a touch of cold which reached me from the
garden with the dew, I tried to discover whether
I loved Pyotr Sergeyitch or not, . . . and fell
asleep unable to reach any conclusion.

And when in the morning I saw quivering
patches of sunlight and the shadows of the lime-
trees on my bed, what had happened yesterday
rose vividly in my memory. Life seemed to me
rich, varied, full of charm. Humming, I dressed
quickly and went out into the garden. . . .

And what happened afterwards? Why—
nothing. In the winter when we lived in town
Pyotr Sergeyitch came to see us from time to time.
Country acquaintances are charming only in the
country and in summer; in the town and in winter
they lose their charm. When you pour out tea
for them in the town it seems as though they are
wearing other people's coats, and as though they
stirred their tea too long. In the town, too, Pyotr
Sergeyitch spoke sometimes of love, but the effect
was not at all the same as in the country. In the
town we were more vividly conscious of the wall
that stood between us: I had rank and wealth,
while he was poor, and he was not even a noble-
man, but only the son of a deacon and a deputy
public prosecutor; we both of us—I through my
youth and he for some unknown reason—thought
of that wall as very high and thick, and when he
was with us in the town he would criticize aristo-
cratic society with a forced smile, and maintain a

sullen silence when there was anyone else in the drawing-room. There is no wall that cannot be broken through, but the heroes of the modern romance, so far as I know them, are too timid, spiritless, lazy, and oversensitive, and are too ready to resign themselves to the thought that they are doomed to failure, that personal life has disappointed them; instead of struggling they merely criticize, calling the world vulgar and forgetting that their criticism passes little by little into vulgarity.

I was loved, happiness was not far away, and seemed to be almost touching me; I went on living in careless ease without trying to understand myself, not knowing what I expected or what I wanted from life, and time went on and on. . . . People passed by me with their love, bright days and warm nights flashed by, the nightingales sang, the hay smelt fragrant, and all this, sweet and overwhelming in remembrance, passed with me as with everyone rapidly, leaving no trace, was not prized, and vanished like mist. . . . Where is it all ?

My father is dead, I have grown older; everything that delighted me, caressed me, gave me hope—the patter of the rain, the rolling of the thunder, thoughts of happiness, talk of love—all that has become nothing but a memory, and I see before me a flat desert distance; on the plain not one living soul, and out there on the horizon it is dark and terrible. . . .

A ring at the bell. . . . It is Pyotr Sergeyitch. When in the winter I see the trees and remember how green they were for me in the summer I whisper:

" Oh, my darlings !"

And when I see people with whom I spent my spring-time, I feel sorrowful and warm and whisper the same thing.

He has long ago by my father's good offices been transferred to town. He looks a little older, a little fallen away. He has long given up declaring his love, has left off talking nonsense, dislikes his official work, is ill in some way and disillusioned; he has given up trying to get anything out of life, and takes no interest in living. Now he has sat down by the hearth and looks in silence at the fire. . . .

Not knowing what to say I ask him:

" Well, what have you to tell me ?"

" Nothing," he answers.

And silence again. The red glow of the fire plays about his melancholy face.

I thought of the past, and all at once my shoulders began quivering, my head dropped, and I began weeping bitterly. I felt unbearably sorry for myself and for this man, and passionately longed for what had passed away and what life refused us now. And now I did not think about rank and wealth.

I broke into loud sobs, pressing my temples, and muttered:

" My God ! my God ! my life is wasted !"

And he sat and was silent, and did not say to me: " Don't weep." He understood that I must weep, and that the time for this had come.

I saw from his eyes that he was sorry for me; and I was sorry for him, too, and vexed with this timid, unsuccessful man who could not make a life for me, nor for himself.

When I saw him to the door, he was, I fancied, purposely a long while putting on his coat. Twice he kissed my hand without a word, and looked a long while into my tear-stained face. I believe at that moment he recalled the storm, the streaks of rain, our laughter, my face that day; he longed to say something to me, and he would have been glad to say it; but he said nothing, he merely shook his head and pressed my hand. God help him!

After seeing him out, I went back to my study and again sat on the carpet before the fireplace; the red embers were covered with ash and began to grow dim. The frost tapped still more angrily at the windows, and the wind droned in the chimney.

The maid came in and, thinking I was asleep, called my name.

IN EXILE

IN EXILE

OLD SEMYON, nicknamed Canny, and a young Tatar, whom no one knew by name, were sitting on the river-bank by the camp-fire; the other three ferrymen were in the hut. Semyon, an old man of sixty, lean and toothless, but broad-shouldered and still healthy-looking, was drunk; he would have gone in to sleep long before, but he had a bottle in his pocket and he was afraid that the fellows in the hut would ask him for vodka. The Tatar was ill and weary, and wrapping himself up in his rags was describing how nice it was in the Simbirsk province, and what a beautiful and clever wife he had left behind at home. He was not more than twenty-five, and now by the light of the camp-fire, with his pale and sick, mournful face, he looked like a boy.

" To be sure, it is not paradise here," said Canny. " You can see for yourself, the water, the bare banks, clay, and nothing else. . . . Easter has long passed and yet there is ice on the river, and this morning there was snow. . . ."

" It's bad ! it's bad !" said the Tatar, and looked round him in terror.

The dark, cold river was flowing ten paces away; it grumbled, lapped against the hollow clay banks and raced on swiftly towards the far-away sea. Close to the bank there was the dark blur of a big barge, which the ferrymen called a " karbos." Far away on the further bank, lights, dying down and flickering up again, zigzagged like little snakes; they were burning last year's grass. And beyond the little snakes there was darkness again. There little icicles could be heard knocking against the barge. It was damp and cold. . . .

The Tatar glanced at the sky. There were as many stars as at home, and the same blackness all round, but something was lacking. At home in the Simbirsk province the stars were quite different, and so was the sky.

" It's bad ! it's bad !" he repeated.

" You will get used to it," said Semyon, and he laughed. " Now you are young and foolish, the milk is hardly dry on your lips, and it seems to you in your foolishness that you are more wretched than anyone; but the time will come when you will say to yourself: ' I wish no one a better life than mine.' You look at me. Within a week the floods will be over and we shall set up the ferry; you will all go wandering off about Siberia while I shall stay and shall begin going from bank to bank. I've been going like that for twenty-two years, day and night. The pike and the salmon are under the water while I am on the water. And thank God for it, I want nothing; God give everyone such a life."

The Tatar threw some dry twigs on the campfire, lay down closer to the blaze, and said:

" My father is a sick man. When he dies my

mother and wife will come here. They have promised."

"And what do you want your wife and mother for?" asked Canny. "That's mere foolishness, my lad. It's the devil confounding you, damn his soul! Don't you listen to him, the cursed one. Don't let him have his way. He is at you about the women, but you spite him; say, 'I don't want them!' He is on at you about freedom, but you stand up to him and say: 'I don't want it!' I want nothing, neither father nor mother, nor wife, nor freedom, nor post, nor paddock; I want nothing, damn their souls!"

Semyon took a pull at the bottle and went on:

"I am not a simple peasant, not of the working class, but the son of a deacon, and when I was free I lived at Kursk; I used to wear a frock-coat, and now I have brought myself to such a pass that I can sleep naked on the ground and eat grass. And I wish no one a better life. I want nothing and I am afraid of nobody, and the way I look at it is that there is nobody richer and freer than I am. When they sent me here from Russia from the first day I stuck it out; I want nothing! The devil was at me about my wife and about my home and about freedom, but I told him: 'I want nothing.' I stuck to it, and here you see I live well, and I don't complain, and if anyone gives way to the devil and listens to him, if but once, he is lost, there is no salvation for him: he is sunk in the bog to the crown of his head and will never get out.

"It is not only a foolish peasant like you, but

even gentlemen, well-educated people, are lost.
Fifteen years ago they sent a gentleman here from
Russia. He hadn't shared something with his
brothers and had forged something in a will.
They did say he was a prince or a baron, but maybe
he was simply an official—who knows ? Well, the
gentleman arrived here, and first thing he bought
himself a house and land in Muhortinskoe. 'I
want to live by my own work,' says he, ' in the
sweat of my brow, for I am not a gentleman now,'
says he, ' but a settler.' ' Well,' says I, ' God help
you, that's the right thing.' He was a young man
then, busy and careful; he used to mow himself
and catch fish and ride sixty miles on horseback.
Only this is what happened: from the very first
year he took to riding to Gyrino for the post; he
used to stand on my ferry and sigh: ' Ech, Semyon,
how long it is since they sent me any money from
home !' ' You don't want money, Vassily Sergeyitch,' says I. ' What use is it to you ? You
cast away the past, and forget it as though it had
never been at all, as though it had been a dream,
and begin to live anew. Don't listen to the devil,'
says I; ' he will bring you to no good, he'll draw
you into a snare. Now you want money,' says I,
' but in a very little while you'll be wanting something else, and then more and more. If you want
to be happy,' says I, ' the chief thing is not to want
anything. Yes. . . . If,' says I, ' if fate has
wronged you and me cruelly, it's no good asking
for her favour and bowing down to her, but you
despise her and laugh at her, or else she will laugh
at you.' That's what I said to him. . . .

"Two years later I ferried him across to this side, and he was rubbing his hands and laughing. 'I am going to Gyrino to meet my wife,' says he. 'She was sorry for me,' says he; 'she has come. She is good and kind.' And he was breathless with joy. So a day later he came with his wife. A beautiful young lady in a hat; in her arms was a baby girl. And lots of luggage of all sorts. And my Vassily Sergeyitch was fussing round her; he couldn't take his eyes off her and couldn't say enough in praise of her. 'Yes, brother Semyon, even in Siberia people can live!' 'Oh, all right,' thinks I, 'it will be a different tale presently.' And from that time forward he went almost every week to enquire whether money had not come from Russia. He wanted a lot of money. 'She is losing her youth and beauty here in Siberia for my sake,' says he, 'and sharing my bitter lot with me, and so I ought,' says he, 'to provide her with every comfort. . . .'

"To make it livelier for the lady he made acquaintance with the officials and all sorts of riff-raff. And of course he had to give food and drink to all that crew, and there had to be a piano and a shaggy lapdog on the sofa—plague take it ! . . . Luxury, in fact, self-indulgence. The lady did not stay with him long. How could she ? The clay, the water, the cold, no vegetables for you, no fruit. All around you ignorant and drunken people and no sort of manners, and she was a spoilt lady from Petersburg or Moscow. . . . To be sure she moped. Besides, her husband, say what you like, was not a gentleman now, but a settler—not the same rank.

" Three years later, I remember, on the eve of
the Assumption, there was shouting from the
further bank. I went over with the ferry, and
what do I see but the lady, all wrapped up, and
with her a young gentleman, an official. A sledge
with three horses. . . . I ferried them across
here, they got in and away like the wind. They
were soon lost to sight. And towards morning
Vassily Sergeyitch galloped down to the ferry.
' Didn't my wife come this way with a gentleman
in spectacles, Semyon ?' ' She did,' said I; ' you
may look for the wind in the fields !' He galloped
in pursuit of them. For five days and nights he
was riding after them. When I ferried him over
to the other side afterwards, he flung himself on
the ferry and beat his head on the boards of the
ferry and howled. ' So that's how it is,' says I.
I laughed, and reminded him ' people can live even
in Siberia !' And he beat his head harder than
ever. . . .

" Then he began longing for freedom. His wife
had slipped off to Russia, and of course he was
drawn there to see her and to get her away from
her lover. And he took, my lad, to galloping
almost every day, either to the post or to the town
to see the commanding officer; he kept sending in
petitions for them to have mercy on him and let
him go back home; and he used to say that he had
spent some two hundred roubles on telegrams
alone. He sold his land and mortgaged his house
to the Jews. He grew grey and bent, and yellow
in the face, as though he was in consumption. If
he talked to you he would go, khee—khee—khee,

. . . and there were tears in his eyes. He kept
rushing about like this with petitions for eight
years, but now he has grown brighter and more
cheerful again: he has found another whim to give
way to. You see, his daughter has grown up.
He looks at her, and she is the apple of his eye.
And to tell the truth she is all right, good-looking,
with black eyebrows and a lively disposition.
Every Sunday he used to ride with her to church
in Gyrino. They used to stand on the ferry, side
by side, she would laugh and he could not take his
eyes off her. ' Yes, Semyon,' says he, ' people
can live even in Siberia. Even in Siberia there is
happiness. Look,' says he, ' what a daughter I
have got ! I warrant you wouldn't find another
like her for a thousand versts round.' ' Your
daughter is all right,' says I, ' that's true, certainly.' But to myself I thought: ' Wait a bit,
the wench is young, her blood is dancing, she wants
to live, and there is no life here.' And she did
begin to pine, my lad. . . . She faded and faded,
and now she can hardly crawl about. Consumption.

"So you see what Siberian happiness is, damn
its soul ! You see how people can live in Siberia.
. . . He has taken to going from one doctor to
another and taking them home with him. As soon
as he hears that two or three hundred miles away
there is a doctor or a sorcerer, he will drive to
fetch him. A terrible lot of money he has spent
on doctors, and to my thinking he had better have
spent the money on drink. . . . She'll die just
the same. She is certain to die, and then it will

be all over with him. He'll hang himself from grief or run away to Russia—that's a sure thing. He'll run away and they'll catch him, then he will be tried, sent to prison, he will have a taste of the lash. . . ."

" Good ! good !" said the Tatar, shivering with cold.

" What is good ?" asked Canny.

" His wife, his daughter. . . . What of prison and what of sorrow !—anyway, he did see his wife and his daughter. . . . You say, want nothing. But ' nothing ' is bad ! His wife lived with him three years—that was a gift from God. ' Nothing ' is bad, but three years is good. How not understand ?"

Shivering and hesitating, with effort picking out the Russian words of which he knew but few, the Tatar said that God forbid one should fall sick and die in a strange land, and be buried in the cold and dark earth; that if his wife came to him for one day, even for one hour, that for such happiness he would be ready to bear any suffering and to thank God. Better one day of happiness than nothing.

Then he described again what a beautiful and clever wife he had left at home. Then, clutching his head in both hands, he began crying and assuring Semyon that he was not guilty, and was suffering for nothing. His two brothers and an uncle had carried off a peasant's horses, and had beaten the old man till he was half dead, and the commune had not judged fairly, but had contrived a sentence by which all the three brothers were sent to Siberia, while the uncle, a rich man, was left at home.

" You will get used to it !" said Semyon.

The Tatar was silent, and stared with tear-stained eyes at the fire; his face expressed bewilderment and fear, as though he still did not understand why he was here in the darkness and the wet, beside strangers, and not in the Simbirsk province.

Canny lay near the fire, chuckled at something, and began humming a song in an undertone.

" What joy has she with her father ?" he said a little later. " He loves her and he rejoices in her, that's true; but, mate, you must mind your p's and q's with him, he is a strict old man, a harsh old man. And young wenches don't want strictness. They want petting and ha-ha-ha ! and ho-ho-ho ! and scent and pomade. Yes. . . . Ech ! life, life," sighed Semyon, and he got up heavily. "The vodka is all gone, so it is time to sleep. Eh ? I am going, my lad. . . ."

Left alone, the Tatar put on more twigs, lay down and stared at the fire; be began thinking of his own village and of his wife. If his wife could only come for a month, for a day; and then if she liked she might go back again. Better a month or even a day than nothing. But if his wife kept her promise and came, what would he have to feed her on ? Where could she live here ?

" If there were not something to eat, how could she live ?" the Tatar asked aloud.

He was paid only ten kopecks for working all day and all night at the oar ; it is true that travellers gave him tips for tea and for vodka, but the men shared all they received among themselves, and gave nothing to the Tatar, but only laughed at him. And from poverty he was hungry, cold, and frightened. . . . Now, when his whole body was aching and shivering, he ought to go into the hut and lie down to sleep; but he had nothing to cover him there, and it was colder than on the river-bank; here he had nothing to cover him either, but at least he could make up the fire. . . .

In another week, when the floods were quite over and they set the ferry going, none of the ferrymen but Semyon would be wanted, and the Tatar would begin going from village to village begging for alms and for work. His wife was only seventeen; she was beautiful, spoilt, and shy; could she possibly go from village to village begging alms with her face unveiled? No, it was terrible even to think of that. . . .

It was already getting light; the barge, the bushes of willow on the water, and the waves could be clearly discerned, and if one looked round there was the steep clay slope; at the bottom of it the hut thatched with dingy brown straw, and the huts of the village lay clustered higher up. The cocks were already crowing in the village.

The rusty red clay slope, the barge, the river, the strange, unkind people, hunger, cold, illness, perhaps all that was not real. Most likely it was all a dream, thought the Tatar. He felt that he was asleep and heard his own snoring. . . . Of course he was at home in the Simbirsk province, and he had only to call his wife by name for her to answer; and in the next room was his mother.

. . . What terrible dreams there are, though!
What are they for? The Tatar smiled and opened
his eyes. What river was this, the Volga?

Snow was falling.

"Boat!" was shouted on the further side.
"Boat!"

The Tatar woke up, and went to wake his mates
and row over to the other side. The ferrymen
came on to the river-bank, putting on their torn
sheepskins as they walked, swearing with voices
husky from sleepiness and shivering from the cold.
On waking from their sleep, the river, from which
came a breath of piercing cold, seemed to strike
them as revolting and horrible. They jumped
into the barge without hurrying themselves. . . .
The Tatar and the three ferrymen took the long,
broad-bladed oars, which in the darkness looked
like the claws of crabs; Semyon leaned his stomach
against the tiller. The shout on the other side still
continued, and two shots were fired from a revolver,
probably with the idea that the ferrymen were
asleep or had gone to the pot-house in the village.

"All right, you have plenty of time," said
Semyon in the tone of a man convinced that there
was no necessity in this world to hurry—that it
would lead to nothing, anyway.

The heavy, clumsy barge moved away from the
bank and floated between the willow-bushes, and
only the willows slowly moving back showed that
the barge was not standing still but moving. The
ferrymen swung the oars evenly in time; Semyon
lay with his stomach on the tiller, and, describing
a semicircle in the air, flew from one side to the

other. In the darkness it looked as though the
men were sitting on some antediluvian animal
with long paws, and were moving on it through a
cold, desolate land, the land of which one sometimes dreams in nightmares.

They passed beyond the willows and floated out
into the open. The creak and regular splash of
the oars was heard on the further shore, and a
shout came: " Make haste ! make haste !"

Another ten minutes passed, and the barge
banged heavily against the landing-stage.

" And it keeps sprinkling and sprinkling," muttered Semyon, wiping the snow from his face; " and
where it all comes from God only knows."

On the bank stood a thin man of medium height,
in a jacket lined with fox-fur and in a white lambskin cap. He was standing at a little distance
from his horses and not moving; he had a gloomy,
concentrated expression, as though he were trying
to remember something and angry with his un-
trustworthy memory. When Semyon went up to
him and took off his cap, smiling, he said:

" I am hastening to Anastasyevka. My daughter's worse again, and they say that there is a
new doctor at Anastasyevka."

They dragged the carriage on to the barge and
floated back. The man whom Semyon addressed
as Vassily Sergeyitch stood all the time motionless,
tightly compressing his thick lips and staring off
into space; when his coachman asked permission to
smoke in his presence he made no answer, as though
he had not heard. Semyon, lying with his stomach
on the tiller, looked mockingly at him and said:

"Even in Siberia people can live—can li-ive!"

There was a triumphant expression on Canny's face, as though he had proved something and was delighted that things had happened as he had foretold. The unhappy helplessness of the man in the foxskin coat evidently afforded him great pleasure.

"It's muddy driving now, Vassily Sergeyitch," he said when the horses were harnessed again on the bank. "You should have put off going for another fortnight, when it will be drier. Or else not have gone at all. . . . If any good would come of your going—but as you know yourself, people have been driving about for years and years, day and night, and it's always been no use. That's the truth."

Vassily Sergeyitch tipped him without a word, got into his carriage and drove off.

"There, he has galloped off for a doctor!" said Semyon, shrinking from the cold. "But looking for a good doctor is like chasing the wind in the fields or catching the devil by the tail, plague take your soul! What a queer chap, Lord forgive me a sinner!"

The Tatar went up to Canny, and, looking at him with hatred and repulsion, shivering, and mixing Tatar words with his broken Russian, said: "He is good . . . good; but you are bad! You are bad! The gentleman is a good soul, excellent, and you are a beast, bad! The gentleman is alive, but you are a dead carcase. . . . God created man to be alive, and to have joy and grief and sorrow; but you want nothing, so you are not alive, you are stone, clay! A stone wants nothing and you want nothing. You are a stone, and God does not love you, but He loves the gentleman!"

Everyone laughed; the Tatar frowned contemptuously, and with a wave of his hand wrapped himself in his rags and went to the camp-fire. The ferrymen and Semyon sauntered to the hut.

"It's cold," said one ferryman huskily as he stretched himself on the straw with which the damp clay floor was covered.

"Yes, it's not warm," another assented. "It's a dog's life. . . ."

They all lay down. The door was thrown open by the wind and the snow drifted into the hut; nobody felt inclined to get up and shut the door: they were cold, and it was too much trouble.

"I am all right," said Semyon as he began to doze. "I wouldn't wish anyone a better life."

"You are a tough one, we all know. Even the devils won't take you!"

Sounds like a dog's howling came from outside.

"What's that? Who's there?"

"It's the Tatar crying."

"I say. . . . He's a queer one!"

"He'll get u-used to it!" said Semyon, and at once fell asleep.

The others were soon asleep too. The door remained unclosed.

THE CATTLE-DEALERS

THE CATTLE-DEALERS

The long goods train has been standing for hours
in the little station. The engine is as silent as
though its fire had gone out; there is not a soul
near the train or in the station yard.

A pale streak of light comes from one of the
vans and glides over the rails of a siding. In that
van two men are sitting on an outspread cape:
one is an old man with a big grey beard, wearing a
sheepskin coat and a high lambskin hat, somewhat
like a busby; the other a beardless youth in a
threadbare cloth reefer jacket and muddy high
boots. They are the owners of the goods. The
old man sits, his legs stretched out before him,
musing in silence; the young man half reclines and
softly strums on a cheap accordion. A lantern
with a tallow candle in it is hanging on the wall
near them.

The van is quite full. If one glances in through
the dim light of the lantern, for the first moment the
eyes receive an impression of something shapeless,
monstrous, and unmistakably alive, something
very much like gigantic crabs which move their
claws and feelers, crowd together, and noiselessly
climb up the walls to the ceiling; but if one looks
more closely, horns and their shadows, long lean

backs, dirty hides, tails, eyes, begin to stand out in the dusk. They are cattle and their shadows. There are eight of them in the van. Some turn round and stare at the men and swing their tails. Others try to stand or lie down more comfortably. They are crowded. If one lies down the others must stand and huddle closer. No manger, no halter, no litter, not a wisp of hay. . . .*

At last the old man pulls out of his pocket a silver watch and looks at the time: a quarter past two.

"We have been here nearly two hours," he says, yawning. "Better go and stir them up, or we may be here till morning. They have gone to sleep, or goodness knows what they are up to."

The old man gets up and, followed by his long shadow, cautiously gets down from the van into the darkness. He makes his way along beside the train to the engine, and after passing some two dozen vans sees a red open furnace; a human figure sits motionless facing it; its peaked cap, nose, and knees are lighted up by the crimson glow, all the rest is black and can scarcely be distinguished in the darkness.

"Are we going to stay here much longer?" asks the old man.

No answer. The motionless figure is evidently asleep. The old man clears his throat impatiently and, shrinking from the penetrating damp, walks round the engine, and as he does so the brilliant

* On many railway lines, in order to avoid accidents, it is against the regulations to carry hay on the trains, and so live stock are without fodder on the journey.—*Author's Note.*

light of the two engine-lamps dazzles his eyes for an instant and makes the night even blacker to him; he goes to the station.

The platform and steps of the station are wet. Here and there are white patches of freshly fallen melting snow. In the station itself it is light and as hot as a steam-bath. There is a smell of paraffin. Except for the weighing-machine and a yellow seat on which a man wearing a guard's uniform is asleep, there is no furniture in the place at all. On the left are two wide-open doors. Through one of them the telegraphic apparatus and a lamp with a green shade on it can be seen; through the other, a small room, half of it taken up by a dark cupboard. In this room the head guard and the engine-driver are sitting on the window-sill. They are both feeling a cap with their fingers and disputing.

"That's not real beaver, it's imitation," says the engine-driver. "Real beaver is not like that. Five roubles would be a high price for the whole cap, if you care to know!"

"You know a great deal about it, . . . " the head guard says, offended. "Five roubles, indeed! Here, we will ask the merchant. Mr. Malahin," he says, addressing the old man, " what do you say: is this imitation beaver or real?"

Old Malahin takes the cap into his hand, and with the air of a connoisseur pinches the fur, blows on it, sniffs at it, and a contemptuous smile lights up his angry face.

"It must be imitation!" he says gleefully. "Imitation it is."

A dispute follows. The guard maintains that the cap is real beaver, and the engine-driver and Malahin try to persuade him that it is not. In the middle of the argument the old man suddenly remembers the object of his coming.

" Beaver and cap is all very well, but the train's standing still, gentlemen !" he says. " Who is it we are waiting for ? Let us start !"

" Let us," the guard agrees. " We will smoke another cigarette and go on. But there is no need to be in a hurry. . . . We shall be delayed at the next station, anyway !"

" Why should we ?"

" Oh, well. . . . We are too much behind time. . . . If you are late at one station you can't help being delayed at the other stations to let the trains going the opposite way pass. Whether we set off now or in the morning we shan't be number fourteen. We shall have to be number twenty-three."

" And how do you make that out ?"

" Well, there it is."

Malahin looks at the guard, reflects, and mutters mechanically as though to himself:

" God be my judge, I have reckoned it and even jotted it down in a notebook; we have wasted thirty-four hours standing still on the journey. If you go on like this, either the cattle will die, or they won't pay me two roubles for the meat when I do get there. It's not travelling, but ruination."

The guard raises his eyebrows and sighs with an air that seems to say: " All that is unhappily true !" The engine-driver sits silent, dreamily looking at the cap. From their faces one can see that they have a secret thought in common, which they do not utter, not because they want to conceal it, but because such thoughts are much better expressed by signs than by words. And the old man understands. He feels in his pocket, takes out a ten-rouble note, and without preliminary words, without any change in the tone of his voice or the expression of his face, but with the confidence and directness with which probably only Russians give and take bribes, he gives the guard the note. The latter takes it, folds it in four, and without undue haste puts it in his pocket. After that all three go out of the room, and waking the sleeping guard on the way, go on to the platform.

"What weather!" grumbles the head guard, shrugging his shoulders. "You can't see your hand before your face."

"Yes, it's vile weather."

From the window they can see the flaxen head of the telegraph clerk appear beside the green lamp and the telegraphic apparatus; soon after another head, bearded and wearing a red cap, appears beside it—no doubt that of the station-master. The station-master bends down to the table, reads something on a blue form, rapidly passing his cigarette along the lines. . . . Malahin goes to his van.

The young man, his companion, is still half reclining and hardly audibly strumming on the accordion. He is little more than a boy, with no trace of a moustache; his full white face with its broad cheek-bones is childishly dreamy; his eyes

have a melancholy and tranquil look unlike that
of a grown-up person, but he is broad, strong,
heavy and rough like the old man; he does not stir
nor shift his position, as though he is not equal to
moving his big body. It seems as though any
movement he made would tear his clothes and be
so noisy as to frighten both him and the cattle.
From under his big fat fingers that clumsily pick
out the stops and keys of the accordion comes a
steady flow of thin, tinkling sounds which blend
into a simple, monotonous little tune; he listens
to it, and is evidently much pleased with his performance.

A bell rings, but with such a muffled note that
it seems to come from far away. A hurried second
bell soon follows, then a third and the guard's
whistle. A minute passes in profound silence; the
van does not move, it stands still, but vague sounds
begin to come from beneath it, like the crunch of
snow under sledge-runners; the van begins to
shake and the sounds cease. Silence reigns again.
But now comes the clank of buffers, the violent
shock makes the van start and, as it were, give a
lurch forward, and all the cattle fall against one
another.

"May you be served the same in the world to
come," grumbles the old man, setting straight
his cap, which had slipped on the back of his
head from the jolt. "He'll maim all my cattle
like this!"

Yasha gets up without a word, and, taking one
of the fallen beasts by the horns, helps it to get
on to its legs. . . . The jolt is followed by a

stillness again. The sounds of crunching snow come from under the van again, and it seems as though the train had moved back a little.

"There will be another jolt in a minute," says the old man. And the convulsive quiver does, in fact, run along the train, there is a crashing sound and the bullocks fall on one another again.

"It's a job!" says Yasha, listening. "The train must be heavy. It seems it won't move."

"It was not heavy before, but now it has suddenly got heavy. No, my lad, the guard has not gone shares with him, I expect. Go and take him something, or he will be jolting us till morning."

Yasha takes a three-rouble note from the old man and jumps out of the van. The dull thud of his heavy footsteps resounds outside the van and gradually dies away. Stillness. . . . In the next van a bullock utters a prolonged subdued "moo," as though it were singing.

Yasha comes back. A cold damp wind darts into the van.

"Shut the door, Yasha, and we will go to bed," says the old man. "Why burn a candle for nothing?"

Yasha moves the heavy door; there is a sound of a whistle, the engine and the train set off.

"It's cold," mutters the old man, stretching himself on the cape and laying his head on a bundle. "It is very different at home! It's warm and clean and soft, and there is room to say your prayers, but here we are worse off than any pigs. It's four days and nights since I have taken off my boots."

Yasha, staggering from the jolting of the train, opens the lantern and snuffs out the wick with his wet fingers. The light flares up, hisses like a frying-pan and goes out.

" Yes, my lad," Malahin goes on, as he feels Yasha lie down beside him and the young man's huge back huddle against his own, " it's cold. There is a draught from every crack. If your mother or your sister were to sleep here for one night they would be dead by morning. There it is, my lad: you wouldn't study and go to the high school like your brothers, so you must take the cattle with your father. It's your own fault, you have only yourself to blame. . . . Your brothers are asleep in their beds now, they are snug under the bedclothes, but you, the careless and lazy one, are in the same box as the cattle. . . . Yes. . . ."

The old man's words are inaudible in the noise of the train, but for a long time he goes on muttering, sighing and clearing his throat. . . . The cold air in the railway van grows thicker and more stifling. The pungent odour of fresh dung and smouldering candle makes it so repulsive and acrid that it irritates Yasha's throat and chest as he falls asleep. He coughs and sneezes, while the old man, being accustomed to it, breathes with his whole chest as though nothing were amiss, and merely clears his throat.

To judge from the swaying of the van and the rattle of the wheels the train is moving rapidly and unevenly. The engine breathes heavily, snorting out of time with the pulsation of the train, and altogether there is a medley of sounds. The bullocks huddle together uneasily and knock their horns against the walls.

When the old man wakes up, the deep blue sky of early morning is peeping in at the cracks and at the little uncovered window. He feels unbearably cold, especially in the back and the feet. The train is standing still; Yasha, sleepy and morose, is busy with the cattle.

The old man wakes up out of humour. Frowning and gloomy, he clears his throat angrily and looks from under his brows at Yasha, who, supporting a bullock with his powerful shoulder and slightly lifting it, is trying to disentangle its leg.

"I told you last night that the cords were too long," mutters the old man; "but no, 'It's not too long, Daddy.' There's no making you do anything, you will have everything your own way. . . . Blockhead!"

He angrily moves the door open and the light rushes into the van. A passenger train is standing exactly opposite the door, and behind it a red building with a roofed-in platform—a big station with a refreshment bar. The roofs and bridges of the trains, the earth, the sleepers, all are covered with a thin coating of fluffy, freshly fallen snow. In the spaces between the carriages of the passenger train the passengers can be seen moving to and fro, and a red-haired, red-faced gendarme walking up and down; a waiter in a frock-coat and a snow-white shirt-front, looking cold and sleepy, and probably very much dissatisfied with his fate, is running along the platform carrying a glass of tea and two rusks on a tray.

The old man gets up and begins saying his prayers towards the east. Yasha, having finished with the bullock and put down the spade in the corner, stands beside him and says his prayers also. He merely moves his lips and crosses himself; the father prays in a loud whisper and pronounces the end of each prayer aloud and distinctly.

" . . . And the life of the world to come. Amen," the old man says aloud, draws in a breath, and at once whispers another prayer, rapping out clearly and firmly at the end: " . . . and lay calves upon Thy altar !"

After saying his prayers, Yasha hurriedly crosses himself and says: " Five kopecks, please."

And on being given the five-kopeck piece, he takes a red copper teapot and runs to the station for boiling water. Taking long jumps over the rails and sleepers, leaving huge tracks in the feathery snow, and pouring away yesterday's tea out of the teapot, he runs to the refreshment room and jingles his five-kopeck piece against his teapot. From the van the bar-keeper can be seen pushing away the big teapot and refusing to give half of his samovar for five kopecks, but Yasha turns the tap himself and, spreading wide his elbows so as not to be interfered with, fills his teapot with boiling water.

" Damned blackguard !" the bar-keeper shouts after him as he runs back to the railway van.

The scowling face of Malahin grows a little brighter over the tea.

" We know how to eat and drink, but we don't remember our work. Yesterday we could do

nothing all day but eat and drink, and I'll be bound
we forgot to put down what we spent. What a
memory! Lord have mercy on us!"

The old man recalls aloud the expenditure of the
day before, and writes down in a tattered notebook
where and how much he had given to guards,
engine-drivers, oilers. . . .

Meanwhile the passenger train has long ago
gone off, and an engine runs backwards and for-
wards on the empty line, apparently without any
definite object, but simply enjoying its freedom.
The sun has risen and is playing on the snow;
bright drops are falling from the station roof and
the tops of the vans.

Having finished his tea, the old man lazily
saunters from the van to the station. Here in the
middle of the first-class waiting-room he sees
the familiar figure of the guard standing beside the
station-master, a young man with a handsome
beard in a magnificent rough woollen overcoat.
The young man, probably new to his position,
stands in the same place, gracefully shifting
from one foot to the other like a good racehorse,
looks from side to side, salutes everyone that
passes by, smiles and screws up his eyes. . . . He
is red-cheeked, sturdy, and good-humoured; his
face is full of eagerness, and is as fresh as though
he had just fallen from the sky with the feathery
snow. Seeing Malahin, the guard sighs guiltily
and throws up his hands.

"We can't go number fourteen," he says.
"We are very much behind time. Another train
has gone with that number."

The station-master rapidly looks through some forms, then turns his beaming blue eyes upon Malahin, and, his face radiant with smiles and freshness, showers questions on him:

"You are Mr. Malahin? You have the cattle? Eight vanloads? What is to be done now? You are late and I let number fourteen go in the night. What are we to do now?"

The young man discreetly takes hold of the fur of Malahin's coat with two pink fingers, and, shifting from one foot to the other, explains affably and convincingly that such and such numbers have gone already, and that such and such are going, and that he is ready to do for Malahin everything in his power. And from his face it is evident that he is ready to do anything to please not only Malahin, but the whole world—he is so happy, so pleased, and so delighted! The old man listens, and though he can make absolutely nothing of the intricate system of numbering the trains, he nods his head approvingly, and he, too, puts two fingers on the soft wool of the rough coat. He enjoys seeing and hearing the polite and genial young man. To show goodwill on his side also, he takes out a ten-rouble note and, after a moment's thought, adds a couple of rouble notes to it, and gives them to the station-master. The latter takes them, puts his finger to his cap, and gracefully thrusts them into his pocket.

"Well, gentlemen, can't we arrange it like this?" he says, kindled by a new idea that has flashed on him. "The troop train is late, . . . as you see, it is not here, . . . so why shouldn't you go as the troop train ?* And I will let the troop train go as twenty-eight. Eh ?"

" If you like," agrees the guard.

"Excellent !" the station-master says, delighted. "In that case there is no need for you to wait here; you can set off at once. I'll despatch you immediately. Excellent !"

He salutes Malahin and runs off to his room, reading forms as he goes. The old man is very much pleased by the conversation that has just taken place; he smiles and looks about the room as though looking for something else agreeable.

"We'll have a drink, though," he says, taking the guard's arm.

"It seems a little early for drinking."

"No, you must let me treat you to a glass in a friendly way."

They both go to the refreshment bar. After having a drink the guard spends a long time selecting something to eat.

He is a very stout, elderly man, with a puffy and discoloured face. His fatness is unpleasant, flabby-looking, and he is sallow as people are who drink too much and sleep irregularly.

"And now we might have a second glass," says Malahin. "It's cold now, it's no sin to drink. Please take some. So I can rely upon you, Mr. Guard, that there will be no hindrance or unpleasantness for the rest of the journey. For you know in moving cattle every hour is precious.

* The train destined especially for the transport of troops is called the troop train ; when there are no troops it takes goods, and goes more rapidly than ordinary goods train.— *Author's Note.*

To-day meat is one price; and to-morrow, look you, it will be another. If you are a day or two late and don't get your price, instead of a profit you get home—excuse my saying it—without your breeches. Pray take a little. . . . I rely on you, and as for standing you something or what you like, I shall be pleased to show you my respect at any time."

After having fed the guard, Malahin goes back to the van.

" I have just got hold of the troop train," he says to his son. " We shall go quickly. The guard says if we go all the way with that number we shall arrive at eight o'clock to-morrow evening. If one does not bestir oneself, my boy, one gets nothing. . . . That's so. . . . So you watch and learn. . . ."

After the first bell a man with a face black with soot, in a blouse and filthy frayed trousers hanging very slack, comes to the door of the van. This is the oiler, who had been creeping under the carriages and tapping the wheels with a hammer.

" Are these your vans of cattle ?" he asks.

" Yes. Why ?"

" Why, because two of the vans are not safe. They can't go on, they must stay here to be repaired."

" Oh, come, tell us another ! You simply want a drink, to get something out of me. . . . You should have said so."

" As you please, only it is my duty to report it at once."

Without indignation or protest, simply, almost

mechanically, the old man takes two twenty-kopeck
pieces out of his pocket and gives them to the oiler.
He takes them very calmly, too, and looking good-
na uredly at the old man enters into conversation.

"You are going to sell your cattle, I suppose.
. . . It's good business!"

Malahin sighs and, looking calmly at the oiler's
black face, tells him that trading in cattle used
certainly to be profitable, but now it has become
a risky and losing business.

"I have a mate here," the oiler interrupts him.
"You merchant gentlemen might make him a
little present. . . ."

Malahin gives something to the mate too.   The
troop train goes quickly and the waits at the
stations are comparatively short.   The old man
is pleased.   The pleasant impression made by the
young man in the rough overcoat has gone deep,
the vodka he has drunk slightly clouds his brain,
the weather is magnificent, and everything seems
to be going well.   He talks without ceasing, and
at every stopping place runs to the refreshment
bar.   Feeling the need of a listener, he takes with
him first the guard, and then the engine-driver,
and does not simply drink, but makes a long business of it, with suitable remarks and clinking of
glasses.

"You have your job and we have ours," he says
with an affable smile.   "May God prosper us
and you, and not our will but His be done."

The vodka gradually excites him and he is
worked up to a great pitch of energy.   He wants
to bestir himself, to fuss about, to make enquiries,

to talk incessantly. At one minute he fumbles
in his pockets and bundles and looks for some form.
Then he thinks of something and cannot remember
it; then takes out his pocket-book, and with no
sort of object counts over his money. He bustles
about, sighs and groans, clasps his hands. . . .
Laying out before him the letters and telegrams
from the meat salesmen in the city, bills, post-
office and telegraphic receipt forms, and his notebook, he reflects aloud and insists on Yasha's
listening.

And when he is tired of reading over forms and
talking about prices, he gets out at the stopping
places, runs to the vans where his cattle are, does
nothing, but simply clasps his hands and exclaims
in horror.

"Oh, dear! oh, dear!" he says in a complaining
voice. "Holy Martyr Vlassy! Though they are
bullocks, though they are beasts, yet they want
to eat and drink as men do. . . . It's four days
and nights since they have drunk or eaten. Oh,
dear! oh, dear!"

Yasha follows him and does what he is told like
an obedient son. He does not like the old man's
frequent visits to the refreshment bar. Though
he is afraid of his father, he cannot refrain from
remarking on it.

"So you have begun already!" he says, looking
sternly at the old man. "What are you rejoicing
at? Is it your name-day or what?"

"Don't you dare teach your father."

"Fine goings on!"

When he has not to follow his father along the

other vans Yasha sits on the cape and strums on the accordion. Occasionally he gets out and walks lazily beside the train; he stands by the engine and turns a prolonged, unmoving stare on the wheels or on the workmen tossing blocks of wood into the tender; the hot engine wheezes, the falling blocks come down with the mellow, hearty thud of fresh wood; the engine-driver and his assistant, very phlegmatic and imperturbable persons, perform incomprehensible movements and don't hurry themselves. After standing for a while by the engine, Yasha saunters lazily to the station; here he looks at the eatables in the refreshment bar, reads aloud some quite uninteresting notice, and goes back slowly to the cattle van. His face expresses neither boredom nor desire; apparently he does not care where he is, at home, in the van, or by the engine.

Towards evening the train stops near a big station. The lamps have only just been lighted along the line; against the blue background in the fresh limpid air the lights are bright and pale like stars; they are only red and glowing under the station roof, where it is already dark. All the lines are loaded up with carriages, and it seems that if another train came in there would be no place for it. Yasha runs to the station for boiling water to make the evening tea. Well-dressed ladies and high-school boys are walking on the platform. If one looks into the distance from the platform there are far-away lights twinkling in the evening dusk on both sides of the station—that is the town. What town? Yasha does not care to know. He sees only the dim lights and wretched buildings beyond the station, hears the cabmen shouting, feels a sharp, cold wind on his face, and imagines that the town is probably disagreeable, uncomfortable, and dull.

While they are having tea, when it is quite dark and a lantern is hanging on the wall again as on the previous evening, the train quivers from a slight shock and begins moving backwards. After going a little way it stops; they hear indistinct shouts, someone sets the chains clanking near the buffers, and shouts, "Ready!" The train moves and goes forward. Ten minutes later it is dragged back again.

Getting out of the van, Malahin does not recognize his train. His eight vans of bullocks are standing in the same row with some trolleys which were not a part of the train before. Two or three of these are loaded with rubble and the others are empty. The guards running to and fro on the platform are strangers. They give unwilling and indistinct answers to his questions. They have no thoughts to spare for Malahin; they are in a hurry to get the train together so as to finish as soon as possible and be back in the warmth.

" What number is this ?" asks Malahin.

" Number eighteen."

" And where is the troop train ? Why have you taken me off the troop train ?"

Getting no answer, the old man goes to the station. He looks first for the familiar figure of the head guard and, not finding him, goes to the station-master. The station-master is sitting at a table in his own room, turning over a bundle of forms. He is busy, and affects not to see the newcomer. His appearance is impressive: a cropped black head, prominent ears, a long hooked nose, a swarthy face; he has a forbidding and, as it were, offended expression. Malahin begins making his complaint at great length.

"What?" queries the station-master. "How is this?" he leans against the back of his chair and goes on, growing indignant. "What is it? and why shouldn't you go by number eighteen? Speak more clearly, I don't understand! How is it? Do you want me to be everywhere at once?"

He showers questions on him, and for no apparent reason grows sterner and sterner. Malahin is already feeling in his pocket for his pocket-book, but in the end the station-master, aggrieved and indignant, for some unknown reason jumps up from his seat and runs out of the room. Malahin shrugs his shoulders, and goes out to look for someone else to speak to.

From boredom or from a desire to put the finishing stroke to a busy day, or simply that a window with the inscription " Telegraph !" on it catches his eye, he goes to the window and expresses a desire to send off a telegram. Taking up a pen, he thinks for a moment, and writes on a blue form: " Urgent. Traffic Manager. Eight vans of live stock. Delayed at every station. Kindly send an express number. Reply paid. Malahin."

Having sent off the telegram, he goes back to the station-master's room. There he finds, sitting on

a sofa covered with grey cloth, a benevolent-look-
ing gentleman in spectacles and a cap of racoon
fur; he is wearing a peculiar overcoat very much
like a lady's, edged with fur, with frogs and slashed
sleeves. Another gentleman, dried-up and sinewy,
wearing the uniform of a railway inspector, stands
facing him.

" Just think of it," says the inspector, addressing
the gentleman in the queer overcoat. " I'll tell
you an incident that really is A1! The Z. railway
line in the coolest possible way stole three hundred
trucks from the N. line. It's a fact, sir! I swear
it! They carried them off, repainted them, put
their letters on them, and that's all about it.
The N. line sends its agents everywhere, they hunt
and hunt. And then—can you imagine it?—
the Company happen to come upon a broken-down
carriage of the Z. line. They repair it at their
depot, and all at once, bless my soul! see their own
mark on the wheels. What do you say to that?
Eh? If I did it they would send me to Siberia,
but the railway companies simply snap their
fingers at it!"

It is pleasant to Malahin to talk to educated,
cultured people. He strokes his beard and joins
in the conversation with dignity.

" Take this case, gentlemen, for instance," he
says. " I am transporting cattle to X. Eight
vanloads. Very good. . . . Now let us say
they charge me for each vanload as a weight of ten
tons; eight bullocks don't weigh ten tons, but much
less, yet they don't take any notice of that. . . ."

At that instant Yasha walks into the room,

looking for his father. He listens and is about to sit down on a chair, but probably thinking of his weight goes and sits on the window-sill.

"They don't take any notice of that," Malahin goes on, "and charge me and my son the third-class fare, too, forty-two roubles, for going in the van with the bullocks. This is my son Yakov. I have two more at home, but they have gone in for study. Well, and apart from that it is my opinion that the railways have ruined the cattle trade. In old days when they drove them in herds it was better."

The old man's talk is lengthy and drawn out. After every sentence he looks at Yasha as though he would say: "See how I am talking to clever people."

"Upon my word!" the inspector interrupts him. "No one is indignant, no one criticizes. And why? It is very simple. An abomination strikes the eye and arouses indignation only when it is exceptional, when the established order is broken by it. Here, where, saving your presence, it constitutes the long-established programme and forms and enters into the basis of the order itself, where every sleeper on the line bears the trace of it and stinks of it, one too easily grows accustomed to it! Yes, sir!"

The second bell rings, the gentleman in the queer overcoat gets up. The inspector takes him by the arm and, still talking with heat, goes off with him to the platform. After the third bell the station-master runs into his room and sits down at his table.

" Listen; with what number am I to go ?" asks Malahin.

The station-master looks at a form and says indignantly:

" Are you Malahin, eight vanloads ? You must pay a rouble a van and six roubles and twenty kopecks for stamps. You have no stamps. Total, fourteen roubles, twenty kopecks."

Receiving the money, he writes something down, dries it with sand, and, hurriedly snatching up a bundle of forms, goes quickly out of the room.

At ten o'clock in the evening Malahin gets an answer from the traffic manager: " Give precedence."

Reading the telegram through, the old man winks significantly and, very well pleased with himself, puts it in his pocket.

" Here," he says to Yasha, " look and learn."

At midnight his train goes on. The night is dark and cold like the previous one; the waits at the stations are long. Yasha sits on the cape and imperturbably strums on the accordion, while the old man is still more eager to exert himself. At one of the stations he is overtaken by a desire to lodge a complaint. At his request a gendarme sits down and writes:

" *November* 10, 188–.—I, non-commissioned officer of the Z. section of the N. police department of railways, Ilya Tchered, in accordance with article 11 of the statute of May 19, 1871, have drawn up this protocol at the station of X. as herewith follows. . . ."

" What am I to write next ?" asks the gendarme.

Malahin lays out before him forms, postal and telegraph receipts, accounts. . . . He does not know himself definitely what he wants of the gendarme; he wants to describe in the protocol not any separate episode but his whole journey, with all his losses and conversations with stationmasters—to describe it lengthily and vindictively.

" At the station of Z.," he says, " write that the station-master unlinked my vans from the troop train because he did not like my countenance."

And he wants the gendarme to be sure to mention his countenance. The latter listens wearily, and goes on writing without hearing him to the end. He ends his protocol thus :

" The above deposition I, non-commissioned officer Tchered, have written down in this protocol with a view to present it to the head of the Z. section, and have handed a copy thereof to Gavril Malahin."

The old man takes the copy, adds it to the papers with which his side pocket is stuffed, and, much pleased, goes back to his van.

In the morning Malahin wakes up again in a bad humour, but his wrath vents itself not on Yasha but the cattle.

" The cattle are done for !" he grumbles. " They are done for ! They are at the last gasp ! God be my judge ! they will all die. Tfoo !"

The bullocks, who have had nothing to drink for many days, tortured by thirst, are licking the hoarfrost on the walls, and when Malahin goes up to them they begin licking his cold fur jacket. From their clear, tearful eyes it can be seen that they are exhausted by thirst and the jolting of the train, that they are hungry and miserable.

"It's a nice job taking you by rail, you wretched brutes!" mutters Malahin. "I could wish you were dead to get it over! It makes me sick to look at you!"

At midday the train stops at a big station where, according to the regulations, there was drinking water provided for cattle.

Water is given to the cattle, but the bullocks will not drink it: the water is too cold. . . .

*   *   *   *   *

Two more days and nights pass, and at last in the distance in the murky fog the city comes into sight. The journey is over. The train comes to a standstill before reaching the town, near a goods station. The bullocks, released from the van, stagger and stumble as though they were walking on slippery ice.

Having got through the unloading and veterinary inspection, Malahin and Yasha take up their quarters in a dirty, cheap hotel in the outskirts of the town, in the square in which the cattle-market is held. Their lodgings are filthy and their food is disgusting, unlike what they ever have at home; they sleep to the harsh strains of a wretched steam hurdy-gurdy which plays day and night in the restaurant under their lodging.

The old man spends his time from morning till night going about looking for purchasers, and Yasha sits for days in the hotel room, or goes out into the street to look at the town. He sees the filthy square heaped up with dung, the signboards of restaurants, the turreted walls of a monastery in the fog. Sometimes he runs across the street and looks into the grocer's shop, admires the jars of cakes of different colours, yawns, and lazily saunters back to his room. The city does not interest him.

At last the bullocks are sold to a dealer. Malahin hires drovers. The cattle are divided into herds, ten in each, and driven to the other end of the town. The bullocks, exhausted, go with drooping heads through the noisy streets, and look indifferently at what they see for the first and last time in their lives. The tattered drovers walk after them, their heads drooping too. They are bored. . . . Now and then some drover starts out of his brooding, remembers that there are cattle in front of him entrusted to his charge, and to show that he is doing his duty brings a stick down full swing on a bullock's back. The bullock staggers with the pain, runs forward a dozen paces, and looks about him as though he were ashamed at being beaten before people.

After selling the bullocks and buying for his family presents such as they could perfectly well have bought at home, Malahin and Yasha get ready for their journey back. Three hours before the train goes the old man, who has already had a drop too much with the purchaser and so is fussy, goes down with Yasha to the restaurant and sits down to drink tea. Like all provincials, he cannot eat and drink alone: he must have company as fussy and as fond of sedate conversation as himself.

"Call the host !" he says to the waiter; "tell
him I should like to entertain him."

The hotel-keeper, a well-fed man, absolutely
indifferent to his lodgers, comes and sits down to
the table.

"Well, we have sold our stock," Malahin says,
laughing. "I have swapped my goat for a hawk.
Why, when we set off the price of meat was three
roubles ninety kopecks, but when we arrived it
had dropped to three roubles twenty-five. They
tell us we are too late, we should have been here
three days earlier, for now there is not the same
demand for meat, St. Philip's fast has come. . . .
Eh ? It's a nice how-do-you-do ! It meant a
loss of fourteen roubles on each bullock. Yes.
But only think what it costs to bring the stock !
Fifteen roubles carriage, and you must put down
six roubles for each bullock, tips, bribes, drinks,
and one thing and another. . . ."

The hotel-keeper listens out of politeness and
reluctantly drinks tea. Malahin sighs and groans,
gesticulates, jests about his ill-luck, but everything shows that the loss he has sustained does not
trouble him much. He doesn't mind whether he
has lost or gained as long as he has listeners, has
something to make a fuss about, and is not late
for his train.

An hour later Malahin and Yasha, laden with
bags and boxes, go downstairs from the hotel
room to the front door to get into a sledge and
drive to the station. They are seen off by the
hotel-keeper, the waiter, and various women.
The old man is touched. He thrusts ten-kopeck

pieces in all directions, and says in a sing-song voice:

" Good-bye, good health to you ! God grant that all may be well with you. Please God if we are alive and well we shall come again in Lent. Good-bye. Thank you. God bless you !"

Getting into the sledge, the old man spends a long time crossing himself in the direction in which the monastery walls make a patch of darkness in the fog. Yasha sits beside him on the very edge of the seat with his legs hanging over the side. His face as before shows no sign of emotion and ex-presses neither boredom nor desire. He is not glad that he is going home, nor sorry that he has not had time to see the sights of the city.

" Drive on !"

The cabman whips up the horse and, turning round, begins swearing at the heavy and cumber-some luggage.

SORROW

SORROW

THE turner, Grigory Petrov, who had been known for years past as a splendid craftsman, and at the same time as the most senseless peasant in the Galtchinskoy district, was taking his old woman to the hospital. He had to drive over twenty miles, and it was an awful road. A government post driver could hardly have coped with it, much less an incompetent sluggard like Grigory. A cutting cold wind was blowing straight in his face. Clouds of snowflakes were whirling round and round in all directions, so that one could not tell whether the snow was falling from the sky or rising from the earth. The fields, the telegraph posts, and the forest could not be seen for the fog of snow. And when a particularly violent gust of wind swooped down on Grigory, even the yoke above the horse's head could not be seen. The wretched, feeble little nag crawled slowly along. It took all its strength to drag its legs out of the snow and to tug with its head. The turner was in a hurry. He kept restlessly hopping up and down on the front seat and lashing the horse's back.

"Don't cry, Matryona, . . ." he muttered. "Have a little patience. Please God we shall

reach the hospital, and in a trice it will be the right
thing for you. . . .   Pavel Ivanitch will give you
some little drops, or tell them to bleed you; or
maybe his honour will be pleased to rub you with
some sort of spirit—it'll . . . draw it out of your
side. Pavel Ivanitch will do his best. He will
shout and stamp about, but he will do his best. . . .
He is a nice gentleman, affable, God give him
health ! As soon as we get there he will dart out
of his room and will begin calling me names.
'How ? Why so ?' he will cry. 'Why did you
not come at the right time ?   I am not a dog to be
hanging about waiting on you devils all day. Why
did you not come in the morning ? Go away !
Get out of my sight. Come again to-morrow.'
And I shall say: 'Mr. Doctor ! Pavel Ivanitch !
Your honour !' Get on, do ! plague take you, you
devil ! Get on !'"

The turner lashed his nag, and without looking
at the old woman went on muttering to himself:

"' Your honour ! It's true as before God. . . .
Here's the Cross for you, I set off almost before
it was light. How could I be here in time if the
Lord. . . . the Mother of God . . . is wroth, and
has sent such a snowstorm ? Kindly look for
yourself. . . . Even a first-rate horse could not
do it, while mine—you can see for yourself—is not
a horse but a disgrace.' And Pavel Ivanitch will
frown and shout: 'We know you ! You always
find some excuse ! Especially you, Grishka; I
know you of old ! I'll be bound you have stopped
at half a dozen taverns !' And I shall say: ' Your
honour ! am I a criminal or a heathen ? My old

woman is giving up her soul to God, she is dying, and am I going to run from tavern to tavern! What an idea, upon my word! Plague take them, the taverns!' Then Pavel Ivanitch will order you to be taken into the hospital, and I shall fall at his feet. . . . 'Pavel Ivanitch! Your honour, we thank you most humbly! Forgive us fools and anathemas, don't be hard on us peasants! We deserve a good kicking, while you graciously put yourself out and mess your feet in the snow!' And Pavel Ivanitch will give me a look as though he would like to hit me, and will say: 'You'd much better not be swilling vodka, you fool, but taking pity on your old woman instead of falling at my feet. You want a thrashing!' 'You are right there—a thrashing, Pavel Ivanitch, strike me God! But how can we help bowing down at your feet if you are our benefactor, and a real father to us? Your honour! I give you my word, . . . here as before God, . . . you may spit in my face if I deceive you: as soon as my Matryona, this same here, is well again and restored to her natural condition, I'll make anything for your honour that you would like to order! A cigarette-case, if you like, of the best birchwood, . . . balls for croquet, skittles of the most foreign pattern I can turn. . . . I will make anything for you! I won't take a farthing from you. In Moscow they would charge you four roubles for such a cigarette-case, but I won't take a farthing.' The doctor will laugh and say: 'Oh, all right, all right. . . . I see! But it's a pity you are a drunkard. . . .' I know how to manage the gentry, old girl. There isn't

a gentleman I couldn't talk to. Only God grant
we don't get off the road. Oh, how it is blowing !
One's eyes are full of snow."

And the turner went on muttering endlessly.
He prattled on mechanically to get a little relief
from his depressing feelings. He had plenty of
words on his tongue, but the thoughts and
questions in his brain were even more numerous.
Sorrow had come upon the turner unawares,
unlooked-for, and unexpected, and now he could
not get over it, could not recover himself. He
had lived hitherto in unruffled calm, as though
in drunken half-consciousness, knowing neither
grief nor joy, and now he was suddenly aware of
a dreadful pain in his heart. The careless idler
and drunkard found himself quite suddenly in the
position of a busy man, weighed down by anxieties
and haste, and even struggling with nature.

The turner remembered that his trouble had
begun the evening before. When he had come
home yesterday evening, a little drunk as usual, and
from long-established habit had begun swearing and
shaking his fists, his old woman had looked at her
rowdy spouse as she had never looked at him before.
Usually the expression in her aged eyes was that of
a martyr, meek like that of a dog frequently beaten
and badly fed ; this time she had looked at him
sternly and immovably, as saints in the holy pictures or dying people look. From that strange, evil
look in her eyes the trouble had begun. The turner,
stupefied with amazement, borrowed a horse from
a neighbour, and now was taking his old woman
to the hospital in the hope that, by means of

powders and ointments, Pavel Ivanitch would bring
back his old woman's habitual expression.

"I say, Matryona, . . ." the turner muttered,
"if Pavel Ivanitch asks you whether I beat you,
say, 'Never!' and I never will beat you again.
I swear it. And did I ever beat you out of spite?
I just beat you without thinking. I am sorry for
you. Some men wouldn't trouble, but here I am
taking you. . . . I am doing my best. And the
way it snows, the way it snows! Thy Will be
done, O Lord! God grant we don't get off the
road. . . . Does your side ache, Matryona, that
you don't speak? I ask you, does your side ache?"

It struck him as strange that the snow on his
old woman's face was not melting; it was queer
that the face itself looked somehow drawn, and
had turned a pale grey, dingy waxen hue and had
grown grave and solemn.

"You are a fool!" muttered the turner. . . .
"I tell you on my conscience, before God, . . .
and you go and . . . Well, you are a fool! I
have a good mind not to take you to Pavel
Ivanitch!"

The turner let the reins go and began thinking.
He could not bring himself to look round at his
old woman: he was frightened. He was afraid,
too, of asking her a question and not getting an
answer. At last, to make an end of uncertainty,
without looking round he felt his old woman's
cold hand. The lifted hand fell like a log.

"She is dead, then! What a business!"

And the turner cried. He was not so much sorry
as annoyed. He thought how quickly everything

passes in this world! His trouble had hardly begun when the final catastrophe had happened. He had not had time to live with his old woman, to show her he was sorry for her before she died. He had lived with her for forty years, but those forty years had passed by as it were in a fog. What with drunkenness, quarrelling, and poverty, there had been no feeling of life. And, as though to spite him, his old woman died at the very time when he felt he was sorry for her, that he could not live without her, and that he had behaved dreadfully badly to her.

"Why, she used to go the round of the village," he remembered. "I sent her out myself to beg for bread. What a business! She ought to have lived another ten years, the silly thing; as it is I'll be bound she thinks I really was that sort of man. . . . Holy Mother! but where the devil am I driving? There's no need for a doctor now, but a burial. Turn back!"

Grigory turned back and lashed the horse with all his might. The road grew worse and worse every hour. Now he could not see the yoke at all. Now and then the sledge ran into a young fir-tree, a dark object scratched the turner's hands and flashed before his eyes, and the field of vision was white and whirling again.

"To live over again," thought the turner.

He remembered that forty years ago Matryona had been young, handsome, merry, that she had come of a well-to-do family. They had married her to him because they had been attracted by his handicraft. All the essentials for a happy life had been there, but the trouble was that, just as he had got drunk after the wedding and lay sprawling on the stove, so he had gone on without waking up till now. His wedding he remembered, but of what happened after the wedding—for the life of him he could remember nothing, except perhaps that he had drunk, lain on the stove, and quarrelled. Forty years had been wasted like that.

The white clouds of snow were beginning little by little to turn grey. It was getting dusk.

"Where am I going?" the turner suddenly bethought him with a start. "I ought to be thinking of the burial, and I am on the way to the hospital. . . . It is as though I had gone crazy!"

Grigory turned round again, and again lashed his horse. The little nag strained its utmost and, with a snort, fell into a little trot. The turner lashed it on the back time after time. . . . A knocking was audible behind him, and though he did not look round, he knew it was the dead woman's head knocking against the sledge. And the snow kept turning darker and darker, the wind grew colder and more cutting. . . .

"To live over again!" thought the turner. "I should get a new lathe, take orders, . . . give the money to my old woman. . . ."

And then he dropped the reins. He looked for them, tried to pick them up, but could not—his hands would not work. . . .

"It does not matter," he thought, "the horse will go of itself, it knows the way. I might have a little sleep now. . . . Before the funeral or the requiem it would be as well to get a little rest. . . ."

The turner closed his eyes and dozed. A little later he heard the horse stop; he opened his eyes and saw before him something dark like a hut or a haystack. . . .

He would have got out of the sledge and found out what it was, but he felt overcome by such inertia that it seemed better to freeze than move, and he sank into a peaceful sleep.

He woke up in a big room with painted walls. Bright sunlight was streaming in at the windows. The turner saw people facing him, and his first feeling was a desire to show himself a respectable man who knew how things should be done.

"A requiem, brothers, for my old woman," he said. "The priest should be told. . . ."

"Oh, all right, all right; lie down," a voice cut him short.

"Pavel Ivanitch!" the turner cried in surprise seeing the doctor before him. "Your honour, benefactor!"

He wanted to leap up and fall on his knees before the doctor, but felt that his arms and legs would not obey him.

"Your honour, where are my legs, where are my arms?"

"Say good-bye to your arms and legs. . . . They've been frozen off. Come, come! . . What are you crying for? You've lived your life, and thank God for it! I suppose you have had sixty years of it—that's enough for you! . . ."

"I am grieving. . . . Graciously forgive me! If I could have another five or six years! . . ."

"What for?"

" The horse isn't mine, I must give it back. . . .
I must bury my old woman. . . . How quickly
it is all ended in this world !   Your honour, Pavel
Ivanitch !   A cigarette-case of birchwood of the
best !   I'll turn you croquet balls. . . ."

The doctor went out of the ward with a wave of
his hand.   It was all over with the turner.

ON OFFICIAL DUTY

ON OFFICIAL DUTY

THE deputy examining magistrate and the district doctor were going to an inquest in the village of Syrnya. On the road they were overtaken by a snowstorm; they spent a long time going round and round, and arrived, not at midday, as they had intended, but in the evening when it was dark. They put up for the night at the Zemstvo hut. It so happened that it was in this hut that the dead body was lying—the corpse of the Zemstvo insurance agent, Lesnitsky, who had arrived in Syrnya three days before and, ordering the samovar in the hut, had shot himself, to the great surprise of everyone; and the fact that he had ended his life so strangely, after unpacking his eatables and laying them out on the table, and with the samovar before him, led many people to suspect that it was a case of murder; an inquest was necessary.

In the outer room the doctor and the examining magistrate shook the snow off themselves and knocked it off their boots. And meanwhile the old village constable, Ilya Loshadin, stood by, holding a little tin lamp. There was a strong smell of paraffin.

" Who are you ?" asked the doctor.

" Conshtable, . . ." answered the constable.

He used to spell it "conshtable" when he signed the receipts at the post office.

"And where are the witnesses?"

"They must have gone to tea, your honour."

On the right was the parlour, the travellers' or gentry's room; on the left the kitchen, with a big stove and sleeping-shelves under the rafters. The doctor and the examining magistrate, followed by the constable, holding the lamp high above his head, went into the parlour. Here a still, long body covered with white linen was lying on the floor close to the table-legs. In the dim light of the lamp they could clearly see, besides the white covering, new rubber goloshes, and everything about it was uncanny and sinister: the dark walls, and the silence, and the goloshes, and the stillness of the dead body. On the table stood a samovar, cold long ago; and round it parcels, probably the eatables.

"To shoot oneself in the Zemstvo hut, how tactless!" said the doctor. "If one does want to put a bullet through one's brains, one ought to do it at home in some outhouse."

He sank on to a bench, just as he was, in his cap, his fur coat, and his felt overboots; his fellow-traveller, the examining magistrate, sat down opposite.

"These hysterical, neurasthenic people are great egoists," the doctor went on hotly. "If a neurasthenic sleeps in the same room with you, he rustles his newspaper; when he dines with you, he gets up a scene with his wife without troubling about your presence; and when he feels inclined to shoot himself, he shoots himself in a village in a Zemstvo hut, so as to give the maximum of trouble to everybody. These gentlemen in every circumstance of life think of no one but themselves! That's why the elderly so dislike our 'nervous age.'"

"The elderly dislike so many things," said the examining magistrate, yawning. "You should point out to the elder generation what the difference is between the suicides of the past and the suicides of to-day. In the old days the so-called gentleman shot himself because he had made away with Government money, but nowadays it is because he is sick of life, depressed. . . . Which is better?"

"Sick of life, depressed; but you must admit that he might have shot himself somewhere else."

"Such trouble!" said the constable, "such trouble! It's a real affliction. The people are very much upset, your honour; they haven't slept these three nights. The children are crying. The cows ought to be milked, but the women won't go to the stall—they are afraid . . . for fear the gentleman should appear to them in the darkness. Of course they are silly women, but some of the men are frightened too. As soon as it is dark they won't go by the hut one by one, but only in a flock together. And the witnesses too. . . ."

Dr. Startchenko, a middle-aged man in spectacles with a dark beard, and the examining magistrate Lyzhin, a fair man, still young, who had only taken his degree two years before and looked more like a student than an official, sat in silence, musing. They were vexed that they were late. Now they had to wait till morning, and to stay here for the night, though it was not yet six o'clock; and they had before them a long evening, a dark night, boredom, uncomfortable beds, beetles, and cold in the morning; and listening to the blizzard that howled in the chimney and in the loft, they both thought how unlike all this was the life which they would have chosen for themselves and of which they had once dreamed, and how far away they both were from their contemporaries, who were at that moment walking about the lighted streets in town without noticing the weather, or were getting ready for the theatre, or sitting in their studies over a book. Oh, how much they would have given now only to stroll along the Nevsky Prospect, or along Petrovka in Moscow, to listen to decent singing, to sit for an hour or so in a restaurant !

"Oo-oo-oo-oo !" sang the storm in the loft, and something outside slammed viciously, probably the signboard on the hut. "Oo-oo-oo-oo !"

"You can do as you please, but I have no desire to stay here," said Startchenko, getting up. "It's not six yet, it's too early to go to bed; I am off. Von Taunitz lives not far from here, only a couple of miles from Syrnya. I shall go to see him and spend the evening there. Constable, run and tell my coachman not to take the horses out. And what are you going to do ?" he asked Lyzhin.

"I don't know; I expect I shall go to sleep."

The doctor wrapped himself in his fur coat and went out. Lyzhin could hear him talking to the coachman and the bells beginning to quiver on the frozen horses. He drove off.

"It is not nice for you, sir, to spend the night in here," said the constable; "come into the other room. It's dirty, but for one night it won't matter. I'll get a samovar from a peasant and heat it directly. I'll heap up some hay for you, and then you go to sleep, and God bless you, your honour."

A little later the examining magistrate was sitting in the kitchen drinking tea, while Loshadin, the constable, was standing at the door talking. He was an old man about sixty, short and very thin, bent and white, with a naïve smile on his face and watery eyes; and he kept smacking with his lips as though he were sucking a sweetmeat. He was wearing a short sheepskin coat and high felt boots, and held his stick in his hands all the time. The youth of the examining magistrate aroused his compassion, and that was probably why he addressed him familiarly.

"The elder gave orders that he was to be informed when the police superintendent or the examining magistrate came," he said, "so I suppose I must go now. . . . It's nearly three miles to the *volost*, and the storm, the snowdrifts, are something terrible—maybe one won't get there before midnight. Ough! how the wind roars!"

"I don't need the elder," said Lyzhin. "There is nothing for him to do here."

He looked at the old man with curiosity, and asked:

"Tell me, grandfather, how many years have you been constable?"

"How many? Why, thirty years. Five years

after the Freedom I began going as constable, that's how I reckon it. And from that time I have been going every day since. Other people have holidays, but I am always going. When it's Easter and the church bells are ringing and Christ has risen, I still go about with my bag—to the treasury, to the post, to the police superintendent's lodgings, to the rural captain, to the tax inspector, to the municipal office, to the gentry, to the peasants, to all orthodox Christians. I carry parcels, notices, tax papers, letters, forms of different sorts, circulars, and to be sure, kind gentleman, there are all sorts of forms nowadays, so as to note down the numbers— yellow, white, and red—and every gentleman or priest or well-to-do peasant must write down a dozen times in the year how much he has sown and harvested, how many quarters or poods he has of rye, how many of oats, how many of hay, and what the weather's like, you know, and insects, too, of all sorts. To be sure, you can write what you like, it's only a regulation, but one must go and give out the notices and then go again and collect them. Here, for instance, there's no need to cut open the gentleman; you know yourself it's a silly thing, it's only dirtying your hands, and here you have been put to trouble, your honour; you have come because it's the regulation; you can't help it. For thirty years I have been going round according to regulation. In the summer it is all right, it is warm and dry; but in winter and autumn it's uncomfortable. At times I have been almost drowned and almost frozen; all sorts of things have happened—wicked people set on me in the forest and took away my bag; I have been beaten, and I have been before a court of law."

"What were you accused of?"

"Of fraud."

"How do you mean?"

"Why, you see, Hrisanf Grigoryev, the clerk, sold the contractor some boards belonging to some-one else—cheated him, in fact. I was mixed up in it. They sent me to the tavern for vodka; well, the clerk did not share with me—did not even offer me a glass; but as through my poverty I was—in appearance, I mean—not a man to be relied upon, not a man of any worth, we were both brought to trial; he was sent to prison, but, praise God! I was acquitted on all points. They read a notice, you know, in the court. And they were all in uniforms —in the court, I mean. I can tell you, your honour, my duties for anyone not used to them are terrible, absolutely killing; but to me it is nothing. In fact, my feet ache when I am not walking. And at home it is worse for me. At home one has to heat the stove for the clerk in the *volost* office, to fetch water for him, to clean his boots."

"And what wages do you get?" Lyzhin asked.

"Eighty-four roubles a year."

"I'll bet you get other little sums coming in. You do, don't you?"

"Other little sums? No, indeed! Gentlemen nowadays don't often give tips. Gentlemen nowadays are strict, they take offence at any-thing. If you bring them a notice they are offended, if you take off your cap before them they

are offended. 'You have come to the wrong
entrance,' they say. 'You are a drunkard,' they
say. 'You smell of onion; you are a blockhead;
you are the son of a bitch.' There are kind-hearted
ones, of course; but what does one get from them ?
They only laugh and call one all sorts of names.
Mr. Altuhin, for instance, he is a good-natured
gentleman; and if you look at him he seems sober
and in his right mind, but so soon as he sees me he
shouts and does not know what he means himself.
He gave me such a name. 'You,' said he, . . .''
The constable uttered some word, but in such a low
voice that it was impossible to make out what he
said.

"What ?" Lyzhin asked. "Say it again."

"'Administration,'" the constable repeated
aloud. "He has been calling me that for a long
while, for the last six years. 'Hullo, Administration !' But I don't mind; let him, God bless him !
Sometimes a lady will send one a glass of vodka
and a bit of pie, and one drinks to her health. But
peasants give more; peasants are more kind-
hearted, they have the fear of God in their hearts:
one will give a bit of bread, another a drop of
cabbage soup, another will stand one a glass. The
village elders treat one to tea in the tavern. Here
the witnesses have gone to their tea. 'Loshadin,'
they said, 'you stay here and keep watch for us,'
and they gave me a kopeck each. You see, they
are frightened, not being used to it, and yesterday
they gave me fifteen kopecks and offered me a
glass.''

"And you, aren't you frightened ?"

" I am, sir; but of course it is my duty, there is
no getting away from it. In the summer I was
taking a convict to the town, and he set upon me
and gave me such a drubbing! And all around
were fields, forest—how could I get away from
him? It's just the same here. I remember the
gentleman, Mr. Lesnitsky, when he was so high,
and I knew his father and mother. I am from the
village of Nedoshtchotova, and they, the Lesnitsky
family, were not more than three-quarters of a mile
from us and less than that, their ground next to
ours, and Mr. Lesnitsky had a sister, a God-fearing
and tender-hearted lady. Lord keep the soul of
Thy servant Yulya, eternal memory to her! She
was never married, and when she was dying she
divided all her property; she left three hundred
acres to the monastery, and six hundred to the
commune of peasants of Nedoshtchotova to com-
memorate her soul; but her brother hid the will,
they do say burnt it in the stove, and took all this
land for himself. He thought, to be sure, it was
for his benefit; but—nay, wait a bit, you won't
get on in the world through injustice, brother.
The gentleman did not go to confession for twenty
years after. He kept away from the church, to be
sure, and died impenitent. He burst. He was a
very fat man, so he burst lengthways. Then everything was taken from the young master, from
Seryozha, to pay the debts—everything there was.
Well, he had not gone very far in his studies, he
couldn't do anything, and the president of the
Rural Board, his uncle—' I'll take him '—Seryozha,
I mean—thinks he, ' for an agent; let him collect

the insurance, that's not a difficult job,' and the gentleman was young and proud, he wanted to be living on a bigger scale and in better style and with more freedom. To be sure, it was a come-down for him to be jolting about the district in a wretched cart and talking to the peasants; he would walk and keep looking on the ground, looking on the ground and saying nothing; if you called his name right in his ear, ' Sergey Sergeyitch!' he would look round like this, ' Eh ?' and look down on the ground again, and now you see he has laid hands on himself. There's no sense in it, your honour, it's not right, and there's no making out what's the meaning of it, merciful Lord! Say your father was rich and you are poor; it is mortifying, there's no doubt about it, but there, you must make up your mind to it. I used to live in good style, too; I had two horses, your honour, three cows, I used to keep twenty head of sheep; but the time has come, and I am left with nothing but a wretched bag, and even that is not mine but Government property. And now in our Nedoshtchotova, if the truth is to be told, my house is the worst of the lot. Makey had four footmen, and now Makey is a footman himself. Petrak had four labourers, and now Petrak is a labourer himself."

"How was it you became poor?" asked the examining magistrate.

"My sons drink terribly. I could not tell you how they drink, you wouldn't believe it."

Lyzhin listened and thought how he, Lyzhin, would go back sooner or later to Moscow, while this old man would stay here for ever, and would always be walking and walking. And how many times in his life he would come across such battered, unkempt old men, not "men of any worth," in whose souls fifteen kopecks, glasses of vodka, and a profound belief that you can't get on in this life by dishonesty, were equally firmly rooted.

Then he grew tired of listening, and told the old man to bring him some hay for his bed. There was an iron bedstead with a pillow and a quilt in the traveller's room, and it could be fetched in; but the dead man had been lying by it for nearly three days (and perhaps sitting on it just before his death), and it would be disagreeable to sleep upon it now. . . .

"It's only half-past seven," thought Lyzhin, glancing at his watch. "How awful it is!"

He was not sleepy, but having nothing to do to pass away the time, he lay down and covered himself with a rug. Loshadin went in and out several times, clearing away the tea-things; smacking his lips and sighing, he kept tramping round the table; at last he took his little lamp and went out, and, looking at his long, grey-headed, bent figure from behind, Lyzhin thought:

"Just like a magician in an opera."

It was dark. The moon must have been behind the clouds, as the windows and the snow on the window-frames could be seen distinctly.

"Oo-oo-oo-oo !" sang the storm, "Oo-oo-oo-oo!"

"Ho-ho-ly sa-aints !" wailed a woman in the loft, or it sounded like it. "Ho-ho-ly sa-aints !"

" B-booh!" something outside banged against the wall. " Trah !"

The examining magistrate listened: there was no woman up there, it was the wind howling. It was rather cold, and he put his fur coat over his rug. As he got warm he thought how remote all this— the storm, and the hut, and the old man, and the dead body lying in the next room—how remote it all was from the life he desired for himself, and how alien it all was to him, how petty, how uninteresting. If this man had killed himself in Moscow or somewhere in the neighbourhood, and he had had to hold an inquest on him there, it would have been interesting, important, and perhaps he might even have been afraid to sleep in the next room to the corpse. Here, nearly a thousand miles from Moscow, all this was seen somehow in a different light; it was not life, they were not human beings, but something only existing "according to the regulation," as Loshadin said; it would leave not the faintest trace in the memory, and would be forgotten as soon as he, Lyzhin, drove away from Syrnya. The fatherland, the real Russia, was Moscow, Petersburg; but here he was in the provinces, the colonies. When one dreamed of playing a leading part, of becoming a popular figure, of being, for instance, examining magistrate in particularly important cases or prosecutor in a circuit court, of being a society lion, one always thought of Moscow. To live, one must be in Moscow; here one cared for nothing, one grew easily resigned to one's insignificant position, and only expected one thing of life—to get away

quickly, quickly. And Lyzhin mentally moved
about the Moscow streets, went into the familiar
houses, met his kindred, his comrades, and there was
a sweet pang at his heart at the thought that he was
only twenty-six, and that if in five or ten years he
could break away from here and get to Moscow, even
then it would not be too late and he would still have
a whole life before him. And as he sank into un-
consciousness, as his thoughts began to be confused, he imagined the long corridor of the court
at Moscow, himself delivering a speech, his sisters,
the orchestra which for some reason kept droning:
" Oo-oo-oo-oo !   Oo-oo-oo-oo !"

" Booh !   Trah !" sounded again.   " Booh !"

And he suddenly recalled how one day, when he
was talking to the book-keeper in the little office
of the Rural Board, a thin, pale gentleman with
black hair and dark eyes walked in; he had a disagreeable look in his eyes such as one sees in people
who have slept too long after dinner, and it spoilt
his delicate, intelligent profile; and the high boots
he was wearing did not suit him, but looked clumsy.
The book-keeper had introduced him: " This is
our insurance agent."

" So that was Lesnitsky, . . . this same man,"
. . . Lyzhin reflected now.

He recalled Lesnitsky's soft voice, imagined his
gait, and it seemed to him that someone was walking beside him now with a step like Lesnitsky's.

All at once he felt frightened, his head turned
cold.

" Who's there ?" he asked in alarm.

" The conshtable !"

" What do you want here ? "

" I have come to ask, your honour—you said this evening that you did not want the elder, but I am afraid he may be angry.' He told me to go to him. Shouldn't I go ? "

" That's enough, you bother me," said Lyzhin with vexation, and he covered himself up again.

" He may be angry. . . . I'll go, your honour. I hope you will be comfortable," and Loshadin went out.

In the passage there was coughing and subdued voices. The witnesses must have returned.

" We'll let those poor beggars get away early to-morrow, . . ." thought the examining magistrate; " we'll begin the inquest as soon as it is daylight."

He began sinking into forgetfulness when suddenly there were steps again, not timid this time but rapid and noisy. There was the slam of a door, voices, the scratching of a match. . . .

" Are you asleep ? Are you asleep ? " Dr. Startchenko was asking him hurriedly and angrily as he struck one match after another; he was covered with snow, and brought a chill air in with him. " Are you asleep ? Get up ! Let us go to Von Taunitz's. He has sent his own horses for you. Come along. There, at any rate, you will have supper, and sleep like a human being. You see I have come for you myself. The horses are splendid, we shall get there in twenty minutes."

" And what time is it now ? "

" A quarter past ten."

Lyzhin, sleepy and discontented, put on his felt

overboots, his fur-lined coat, his cap and hood, and went out with the doctor. There was not a very sharp frost, but a violent and piercing wind was blowing and driving along the street the clouds of snow which seemed to be racing away in terror: high drifts were heaped up already under the fences and at the doorways. The doctor and the examining magistrate got into the sledge, and the white coachman bent over them to button up the cover. They were both hot.

" Ready !"

They drove through the village. " Cutting a feathery furrow," thought the examining magistrate, listlessly watching the action of the trace-horse's legs. There were lights in all the huts, as though it were the eve of a great holiday: the peasants had not gone to bed because they were afraid of the dead body. The coachman preserved a sullen silence, probably he had felt dreary while he was waiting by the Zemstvo hut, and now he, too, was thinking of the dead man.

"At the Von Taunitz's," said Startchenko, "they all set upon me when they heard that you were left to spend the night in the hut, and asked me why I did not bring you with me."

As they drove out of the village, at the turning the coachman suddenly shouted at the top of his voice: " Out of the way !"

They caught a glimpse of a man: he was standing up to his knees in the snow, moving off the road and staring at the horses. The examining magistrate saw a stick with a crook, and a beard and a bag, and he fancied that it was Loshadin,

and even fancied that he was smiling. He flashed
by and disappeared.

The road ran at first along the edge of the forest,
then along a broad forest clearing; they caught
glimpses of old pines and a young birch copse,
and tall, gnarled young oak-trees standing singly
in the clearings where the wood had lately been
cut; but soon it was all merged in the clouds of
snow. The coachman said he could see the forest;
the examining magistrate could see nothing but
the trace-horse. The wind blew on their backs.

All at once the horses stopped.

"Well, what is it now?" asked Startchenko
crossly.

The coachman got down from the box without
a word and began running round the sledge, tread-
ing on his heels; he made larger and larger circles,
getting further and further away from the sledge,
and it looked as though he were dancing; at last
he came back and began to turn off to the right.

"You've got off the road, eh?" asked Startchenko.

"It's all ri-ight. . . ."

Then there was a little village and not a single
light in it. Again the forest and the fields. Again
they lost the road, and again the coachman got
down from the box and danced round the sledge.
The sledge flew along a dark avenue, flew swiftly
on. And the heated trace-horse's hoofs knocked
against the sledge. Here there was a fearful
roaring sound from the trees, and nothing could be
seen, as though they were flying on into space;
and all at once the glaring light at the entrance

and the windows flashed upon their eyes, and they heard the good-natured, drawn-out barking of dogs. They had arrived.

While they were taking off their fur coats and their felt boots below, " Un Petit Verre de Clicquot " was being played upon the piano overhead, and they could hear the children beating time with their feet. Immediately on going in they were aware of the snug warmth and special smell of the old apartments of a mansion where, whatever the weather outside, life is so warm and clean and comfortable.

"That's capital!" said Von Taunitz, a fat man with an incredibly thick neck and with whiskers, as he shook the examining magistrate's hand. " That's capital ! You are very welcome, delighted to make your acquaintance. We are colleagues to some extent, you know. At one time I was deputy prosecutor ; but not for long, only two years. I came here to look after the estate, and here I have grown old—an old fogey, in fact. You are very welcome," he went on, evidently restraining his voice so as not to speak too loud ; he was going upstairs with his guests. " I have no wife, she's dead. But here, I will introduce my daughters," and turning round, he shouted down the stairs in a voice of thunder : "Tell Ignat to have the sledge ready at eight o'clock to-morrow morning."

His four daughters, young and pretty girls, all wearing grey dresses and with their hair done up in the same style, and their cousin, also young and attractive, with her children, were in the drawing-room. Startchenko, who knew them already, began at once begging them to sing something, and two of the young ladies spent a long time declaring they could not sing and that they had no music; then the cousin sat down to the piano, and with trembling voices, they sang a duet from " The Queen of Spades." Again " Un Petit Verre de Clicquot " was played, and the children skipped about, beating time with their feet. And Startchenko pranced about too.   Everybody laughed.

Then the children said good-night and went off to bed. The examining magistrate laughed, danced a quadrille, flirted, and kept wondering whether it was not all a dream ? The kitchen of the Zemstvo hut, the heap of hay in the corner, the rustle of the beetles, the revolting poverty-stricken surroundings, the voices of the witnesses, the wind, the snow-storm, the danger of being lost; and then all at once this splendid, brightly lighted room, the sounds of the piano, the lovely girls, the curly-headed children, the gay, happy laughter—such a transformation seemed to him like a fairy tale, and it seemed incredible that such transitions were possible at the distance of some two miles in the course of one hour. And dreary thoughts prevented him from enjoying himself, and he kept thinking this was not life here, but bits of life, fragments, that everything here was accidental, that one could draw no conclusions from it; and he even felt sorry for these girls, who were living and would end their lives in the wilds, in a province far away from the centre of culture, where nothing is accidental, but everything is in accordance with reason and law, and where, for instance, every suicide is intelligible, so that one can explain why it has happened and what is its significance in the general scheme of things. He imagined that if the life surrounding him here in the wilds were not intelligible to him, and if he did not see it, it meant that it did not exist at all.

At supper the conversation turned on Lesnitsky.

" He left a wife and child," said Startchenko. " I would forbid neurasthenics and all people whose nervous system is out of order to marry, I would deprive them of the right and possibility of multiplying their kind. To bring into the world nervous, invalid children is a crime."

" He was an unfortunate young man," said Von Taunitz, sighing gently and shaking his head. "What a lot one must suffer and think about before one brings oneself to take one's own life, . . . a young life ! Such a misfortune may happen in any family, and that is awful. It is hard to bear such a thing, insufferable. . . ."

And all the girls listened in silence with grave faces, looking at their father. Lyzhin felt that he, too, must say something, but he couldn't think of anything, and merely said :

" Yes, suicide is an undesirable phenomenon."

He slept in a warm room, in a soft bed covered with a quilt under which there were fine clean sheets, but for some reason did not feel comfortable : perhaps because the doctor and Von Taunitz were, for a long time, talking in the adjoining room, and overhead he heard, through the ceiling and in the stove, the wind roaring just as in the Zemstvo hut, and as plaintively howling : " Oo-oo-oo-oo !"

Von Taunitz's wife had died two years before, and he was still unable to resign himself to his loss and, whatever he was talking about, always mentioned his wife; and there was no trace of a prosecutor left about him now.

"Is it possible that I may some day come to such a condition?" thought Lyzhin, as he fell asleep, still hearing through the wall his host's subdued, as it were bereaved, voice.

The examining magistrate did not sleep soundly. He felt hot and uncomfortable, and it seemed to him in his sleep that he was not at Von Taunitz's, and not in a soft clean bed, but still in the hay at the Zemstvo hut, hearing the subdued voices of the witnesses; he fancied that Lesnitsky was close by, not fifteen paces away. In his dreams he remembered how the insurance agent, black-haired and pale, wearing dusty high boots, had come into the book-keeper's office. "This is our insurance agent. . . ."

Then he dreamed that Lesnitsky and Loshadin the constable were walking through the open country in the snow, side by side, supporting each other; the snow was whirling about their heads, the wind was blowing on their backs, but they walked on, singing: "We go on, and on, and on. . . ."

The old man was like a magician in an opera, and both of them were singing as though they were on the stage:

"We go on, and on, and on! . . . You are in the warmth, in the light and snugness, but we are walking in the frost and the storm, through the deep snow. . . . We know nothing of ease, we know nothing of joy. . . . We bear all the burden of this life, yours and ours. . . . Oo-oo-oo! We go on, and on, and on. . . ."

Lyzhin woke and sat up in bed. What a confused, bad dream! And why did he dream of the constable and the agent together? What nonsense! And now while Lyzhin's heart was throbbing violently and he was sitting on his bed, holding his head in his hands, it seemed to him that there really was something in common between the lives of the insurance agent and the constable. Don't they really go side by side holding each other up? Some tie unseen, but significant and essential, existed between them, and even between them and Von Taunitz and between all men— all men; in this life, even in the remotest desert, nothing is accidental, everything is full of one common idea, everything has one soul, one aim, and to understand it it is not enough to think, it is not enough to reason, one must have also, it seems, the gift of insight into life, a gift which is evidently not bestowed on all. And the unhappy man who had broken down, who had killed himself —the "neurasthenic," as the doctor called him— and the old peasant who spent every day of his life going from one man to another, were only accidental, were only fragments of life for one who thought of his own life as accidental, but were parts of one organism—marvellous and rational— for one who thought of his own life as part of that universal whole and understood it. So thought Lyzhin, and it was a thought that had long lain hidden in his soul, and only now it

IX.   12 was unfolded broadly and clearly to his consciousness.

He lay down and began to drop asleep; and again they were going along together, singing: "We go on, and on, and on. . . . We take from life what is hardest and bitterest in it, and we leave you what is easy and joyful; and sitting at supper, you can coldly and sensibly discuss why we suffer and perish, and why we are not as sound and as satisfied as you."

What they were singing had occurred to his mind before, but the thought was somewhere in the background behind his other thoughts, and flickered timidly like a far-away light in foggy weather. And he felt that this suicide and the peasant's sufferings lay upon his conscience, too; to resign himself to the fact that these people, submissive to their fate, should take up the burden of what was hardest and gloomiest in life—how awful it was ! To accept this, and to desire for himself a life full of light and movement among happy and contented people, and to be continually dreaming of such, means dreaming of fresh suicides of men crushed by toil and anxiety, or of men weak and outcast whom people only talk of sometimes at supper with annoyance or mockery, without going to their help. . . . And again:

"We go on, and on, and on . . ." as though someone were beating with a hammer on his temples.

He woke early in the morning with a headache, roused by a noise; in the next room Von Taunitz was saying loudly to the doctor:

" It's impossible for you to go now. Look what's going on outside. Don't argue, you had better ask the coachman; he won't take you in such weather for a million."

" But it's only two miles," said the doctor in an imploring voice.

" Well, if it were only half a mile. If you can't, then you can't. Directly you drive out of the gates it is perfect hell, you would be off the road in a minute. Nothing will induce me to let you go, you can say what you like."

" It's bound to be quieter towards evening," said the peasant who was heating the stove.

And in the next room the doctor began talking of the rigorous climate and its influence on the character of the Russian, of the long winters which, by preventing movement from place to place, hinder the intellectual development of the people; and Lyzhin listened with vexation to these observations and looked out of window at the snowdrifts which were piled on the fence. He gazed at the white dust which covered the whole visible expanse, at the trees which bowed their heads despairingly to right and then to left, listened to the howling and the banging, and thought gloomily:

" Well, what moral can be drawn from it ? It's a blizzard and that is all about it. . . ."

At midday they had lunch, then wandered aimlessly about the house; they went to the windows.

" And Lesnitsky is lying there," thought Lyzhin, watching the whirling snow, which raced furiously round and round upon the drifts. "Lesnitsky is lying there, the witnesses are waiting. . . ."

They talked of the weather, saying that the snow-storm usually lasted two days and nights, rarely longer. At six o'clock they had dinner, then they played cards, sang, danced; at last they had supper. The day was over, they went to bed.

In the night, towards morning, it all subsided. When they got up and looked out of window, the bare willows with their weakly drooping branches were standing perfectly motionless; it was dull and still, as though Nature now were ashamed of its orgy, of its mad nights, and the licence it had given to its passions. The horses, harnessed tandem, had been waiting at the front door since five o'clock in the morning. When it was fully daylight the doctor and the examining magistrate put on their fur coats and felt boots, and, saying good-bye to their host, went out.

At the steps beside the coachman stood the familiar figure of the conshtable, Ilya Loshadin, with an old leather bag across his shoulder and no cap on his head, covered with snow all over, and his face was red and wet with perspiration. The footman who had come out to help the gentlemen and cover their legs looked at him sternly and said:

"What are you standing here for, you old devil? Get away!"

"Your honour, the people are anxious," said Loshadin, smiling naïvely all over his face, and evidently pleased at seeing at last the people he had waited for so long. "The people are very uneasy, the children are crying. . . . They thought, your honour, that you had gone back to the town again. Show us the heavenly mercy, our benefactors ! . . ."

The doctor and the examining magistrate said nothing, got into the sledge, and drove to Syrnya.

THE FIRST-CLASS PASSENGER

THE FIRST-CLASS PASSENGER

THE FIRST-CLASS PASSENGER

A FIRST-CLASS passenger who had just dined at the station and drunk a little too much lay down on the velvet-covered seat, stretched himself out luxuriously, and sank into a doze. After a nap of no more than five minutes, he looked with oily eyes at his *vis-à-vis*, gave a smirk, and said:

"My father of blessed memory used to like to have his heels tickled by peasant women after dinner. I am just like him, with this difference, that after dinner I always like my tongue and my brains gently stimulated. Sinful man as I am, I like empty talk on a full stomach. Will you allow me to have a chat with you?"

"I shall be delighted," answered the *vis-à-vis*.

"After a good dinner the most trifling subject is sufficient to arouse devilishly great thoughts in my brain. For instance, we saw just now near the refreshment bar two young men, and you heard one congratulate the other on being celebrated. 'I congratulate you,' he said; 'you are already a celebrity and are beginning to win fame.' Evidently actors or journalists of microscopic dimensions. But they are not the point. The question that is occupying my mind at the moment, sir, is exactly what is to be understood by the word *fame* or *celebrity*. What do you think? Pushkin called fame a bright patch on a ragged garment; we all understand it as Pushkin does—that is, more or less subjectively—but no one has yet given a clear, logical definition of the word. . . . I would give a good deal for such a definition!"

"Why do you feel such a need for it?"

"You see, if we knew what fame is, the means of attaining it might also perhaps be known to us," said the first-class passenger, after a moment's thought. "I must tell you, sir, that when I was younger I strove after celebrity with every fibre of my being. To be popular was my craze, so to speak. For the sake of it I studied, worked, sat up at night, neglected my meals. And I fancy, as far as I can judge without partiality, I had all the natural gifts for attaining it. To begin with, I am an engineer by profession. In the course of my life I have built in Russia some two dozen magnificent bridges, I have laid aqueducts for three towns; I have worked in Russia, in England, in Belgium. . . . Secondly, I am the author of several special treatises in my own line. And thirdly, my dear sir, I have from a boy had a weakness for chemistry. Studying that science in my leisure hours, I discovered methods of obtaining certain organic acids, so that you will find my name in all the foreign manuals of chemistry. I have always been in the service, I have risen to the grade of actual civil councillor, and I have an unblemished record. I will not fatigue your attention by enumerating my works and my merits, I will only say that I have done far more than some celebrities.

And yet here I am in my old age, I am getting ready for my coffin, so to say, and I am as celebrated as that black dog yonder running on the embankment."

"How can you tell? Perhaps you are celebrated."

"H'm! Well, we will test it at once. Tell me, have you ever heard the name Krikunov?"

The *vis-à-vis* raised his eyes to the ceiling, thought a minute, and laughed.

"No, I haven't heard it, . . ." he said.

"That is my surname. You, a man of education, getting on in years, have never heard of me —a convincing proof! It is evident that in my efforts to gain fame I have not done the right thing at all: I did not know the right way to set to work, and, trying to catch fame by the tail, got on the wrong side of her."

"What is the right way to set to work?"

"Well, the devil only knows! Talent, you say? Genius? Originality? Not a bit of it, sir! . . . People have lived and made a career side by side with me who were worthless, trivial, and even contemptible compared with me. They did not do onetenth of the work I did, did not put themselves out, were not distinguished for their talents, and did not make an effort to be celebrated, but just look at them! Their names are continually in the newspapers and on men's lips! If you are not tired of listening I will illustrate it by an example. Some years ago I built a bridge in the town K. I must tell you that the dulness of that scurvy little town was terrible. If it had not been for

women and cards I believe I should have gone out
of my mind. Well, it's an old story: I was so
bored that I got into an affair with a singer.
Everyone was enthusiastic about her, the devil
only knows why; to my thinking she was—what
shall I say?—an ordinary, commonplace creature,
like lots of others. The hussy was empty-headed,
ill-tempered, greedy, and what's more, she was a
fool.

" She ate and drank a vast amount, slept till five
o'clock in the afternoon—and I fancy did nothing
else. She was looked upon as a cocotte, and that
was indeed her profession; but when people wanted
to refer to her in a literary fashion, they called
her an actress and a singer. I used to be devoted to
the theatre, and therefore this fraudulent pretence
of being an actress made me furiously indignant.
My young lady had not the slightest right to
call herself an actress or a singer. She was a
creature entirely devoid of talent, devoid of
feeling—a pitiful creature, one may say. As
far as I can judge she sang disgustingly. The
whole charm of her ' art ' lay in her kicking
up her legs on every suitable occasion, and not
being embarrassed when people walked into her
dressing-room. She usually selected translated
vaudevilles, with singing in them, and oppor-
tunities for disporting herself in male attire, in
tights. In fact it was—ough ! Well, I ask your
attention. As I remember now, a public ceremony took place to celebrate the opening of the
newly constructed bridge. There was a religious
service, there were speeches, telegrams, and so on.

I hung about my cherished creation, you know,
all the while afraid that my heart would burst with
the excitement of an author. It's an old story
and there's no need for false modesty, and so I
will tell you that my bridge was a magnificent work!
It was not a bridge but a picture, a perfect delight!
And who would not have been excited when the
whole town came to the opening? 'Oh,' I
thought, 'now the eyes of all the public will be on
me! Where shall I hide myself?' Well, I need
not have worried myself, sir—alas! Except the
official personages, no one took the slightest notice
of me. They stood in a crowd on the river-bank,
gazed like sheep at the bridge, and did not concern
themselves to know who had built it. And it
was from that time, by the way, that I began to
hate our estimable public—damnation take them!
Well, to continue. All at once the public became
agitated; a whisper ran through the crowd, . . .
a smile came on their faces, their shoulders began
to move. 'They must have seen me,' I thought.
A likely idea! I looked, and my singer, with a
train of young scamps, was making her way through
the crowd. The eyes of the crowd were hurriedly
following this procession. A whisper began in
a thousand voices: 'That's so-and-so. . . .
Charming! Bewitching!' Then it was they
noticed me. . . . A couple of young milksops,
local amateurs of the scenic art, I presume, looked
at me, exchanged glances, and whispered: 'That's
her lover!' How do you like that? And an unprepossessing individual in a top-hat, with a chin
that badly needed shaving, hung round me, shift-

ing from one foot to the other, then turned to me
with the words:

" ' Do you know who that lady is, walking on
the other bank ? That's so-and-so. . . . Her
voice is beneath all criticism, but she has a most
perfect mastery of it ! . . .'

" ' Can you tell me,' I asked the unprepossessing
individual, ' who built this bridge ?'

" ' I really don't know,' answered the individual;
' some engineer, I expect.'

" ' And who built the cathedral in your town ?'
I asked again.

" ' I really can't tell you.'

" Then I asked him who was considered the
best teacher in K., who the best architect, and to
all my questions the unprepossessing individual
answered that he did not know.

" ' And tell me, please,' I asked in conclusion,
' with whom is that singer living ?'

" ' With some engineer called Krikunov.'

" Well, how do you like that, sir ? But to
proceed. There are no minnesingers or bards
nowadays, and celebrity is created almost exclu-
sively by the newspapers. The day after the dedication of the bridge, I greedily snatched up the local
Messenger, and looked for myself in it. I spent a
long time running my eyes over all the four pages,
and at last there it was—hurrah ! I began reading:
' Yesterday in beautiful weather, before a vast
concourse of people, in the presence of His Excellency the Governor of the province, so-and-so,
and other dignitaries, the ceremony of the dedication of the newly constructed bridge took place,'

and so on. . . .   Towards the end: ' Our talented
actress so-and-so, the favourite of the K. public,
was present at the dedication, looking very beautiful.   I need not say that her arrival created a
sensation.   The star was wearing . . .' and so
on.   They might have given me one word !   Half
a word.   Petty as it seems, I actually cried with
vexation !

" I consoled myself with the reflection that the
provinces are stupid, and one could expect nothing
of them, and for celebrity one must go to the intellectual centres—to Petersburg and to Moscow.
And as it happened, at that very time there was
a work of mine in Petersburg which I had sent in
for a competition.   The date on which the result
was to be declared was at hand.

" I took leave of K. and went to Petersburg.   It
is a long journey from K. to Petersburg, and that
I might not be bored on the journey I took a
reserved compartment and—well—of course, I
took my singer.   We set off, and all the way we
were eating, drinking champagne, and—tra-la-la !
But behold, at last we reach the intellectual centre.
I arrived on the very day the result was declared,
and had the satisfaction, my dear sir, of celebrating
my own success: my work received the first prize.
Hurrah !   Next day I went out along the Nevsky
and spent seventy kopecks on various newspapers.
I hastened to my hotel room, lay down on the sofa,
and, controlling a quiver of excitement, made haste
to read.   I ran through one newspaper—nothing.
I ran through a second—nothing either; my God !
At last, in the fourth, I lighted upon the following

paragraph: ' Yesterday the well-known provincial
actress so-and-so arrived by express in Petersburg.
We note with pleasure that the climate of the South
has had a beneficial effect on our fair friend; her
charming stage appearance . . .' and I don't
remember the rest ! Much lower down than that
paragraph I found, printed in the smallest type
' The first prize in the competition was adjudged
to an engineer called so-and-so.' That was all !
And to make things better, they even misspelt
my name : instead of Krikunov it was Kirkunov.
So much for your intellectual centre ! But that
was not all. . . . By the time I left Petersburg.
a month later, all the newspapers were vying
with one another in discussing ' our incomparable,
divine, highly talented actress,' and my mistress
was referred to, not by her surname, but by her
Christian name and her father's. . . .

"Some years later I was in Moscow. I was summoned there by a letter, in the mayor's own
handwriting, to undertake a work for which
Moscow, in its newspapers, had been clamouring
for over a hundred years. In the intervals of my
work I delivered five public lectures, with a phil-
anthropic object, in one of the museums there.
One would have thought that was enough to make
one known to the whole town for three days at
least. wouldn't one ? But, alas ! not a single
Moscow gazette said a word about me. There
was something about houses on fire, about an
operetta, sleeping town councillors, drunken shop-
keepers—about everything; but about my work,
my plans, my lectures—mum. And a nice set

they are in Moscow ! I got into a tram. . . . It was packed full; there were ladies and military men and students of both sexes, creatures of all sorts in couples.

" ' I am told the town council has sent for an engineer to plan such and such a work !' I said to my neighbour, so loudly that all the tram could hear. ' Do you know the name of the engineer ?'

" My neighbour shook his head. The rest of the public took a cursory glance at me, and in all their eyes I read: ' I don't know.'

" ' I am told that there is someone giving lectures in such and such a museum ?' I persisted, trying to get up a conversation. ' I hear it is interesting.'

"No one even nodded. Evidently they had not all of them heard of the lectures, and the ladies were not even aware of the existence of the museum. All that would not have mattered, but imagine, my dear sir, the people suddenly leaped to their feet and struggled to the windows. What was it ? What was the matter ?

" ' Look, look !' my neighbour nudged me. ' Do you see that dark man getting into that cab ? That's the famous runner, King !'

"And the whole tram began talking breathlessly of the runner who was then absorbing the brains of Moscow.

I could give you ever so many other examples, but I think that is enough. Now let us assume that I am mistaken about myself, that I am a wretchedly boastful and incompetent person; but apart from myself I might point to many of

my contemporaries, men remarkable for their
talent and industry, who have nevertheless died
unrecognized. Are Russian navigators, chemists,
physicists, mechanicians, and agriculturists popular
with the public ? Do our cultivated masses know
anything of Russian artists, sculptors, and literary
men ? Some old literary hack, hard-working and
talented, will wear away the doorstep of the pub-
lishers' offices for thirty-three years, cover reams
of paper, be had up for libel twenty times, and yet
not step beyond his ant-heap. Can you mention
to me a single representative of our literature who
would have become celebrated if the rumour had
not been spread over the earth that he had been
killed in a duel, gone out of his mind, been sent
into exile, or had cheated at cards ?"

The first-class passenger was so excited that he
dropped his cigar out of his mouth and got up.

"Yes," he went on fiercely, "and side by side
with these people I can quote you hundreds of
all sorts of singers, acrobats, buffoons, whose
names are known to every baby. Yes !"

The door creaked, there was a draught, and an
individual of forbidding aspect, wearing an Inver-
ness coat, a top-hat, and blue spectacles, walked
into the carriage. The individual looked round
at the seats, frowned, and went on further.

"Do you know who that is ?" there came a
timid whisper from the furthest corner of the compartment. "That is N. N., the famous Tula
cardsharper who was had up in connection with
the Y. bank affair."

"There you are !" laughed the first-class pas-

senger. " He knows a Tula cardsharper, but ask
him whether he knows Semiradsky, Tchaykovsky,
or Solovyov the philosopher—he'll shake his head.
. . . It's swinish !"

Three minutes passed in silence.

" Allow me in my turn to ask you a question,"
said the *vis-à-vis* timidly, clearing his throat.
" Do you know the name of Pushkov ?"

" Pushkov ? H'm ! Pushkov. . . . No, I
don't know it !"

" That is my name, . . ." said the *vis-à-vis*,
overcome with embarrassment. " Then you don't
know it ? And yet I have been a professor at one
of the Russian universities for thirty-five years,
. . . a member of the Academy of Sciences, . . .
have published more than one work. . . ."

The first-class passenger and the *vis-à-vis* looked
at each other and burst out laughing.

A TRAGIC ACTOR

A TRAGIC ACTOR

It was the benefit night of Fenogenov, the tragic actor. They were acting "Prince Serebryany." The tragedian himself was playing Vyazemsky; Limonadov, the stage manager, was playing Morozov; Madame Beobahtov, Elena. The performance was a grand success. The tragedian accomplished wonders indeed. When he was carrying off Elena, he held her in one hand above his head as he dashed across the stage. He shouted, hissed, banged with his feet, tore his coat across his chest. When he refused to fight Morozov, he trembled all over as nobody ever trembles in reality, and gasped loudly. The theatre shook with applause. There were endless calls. Fenogenov was presented with a silver cigarette-case and a bouquet tied with long ribbons. The ladies waved their handkerchiefs and urged their men to applaud, many shed tears. . . . But the one who was the most enthusiastic and most excited was Masha, daughter of Sidoretsky the police captain. She was sitting in the first row of the stalls beside her papa; she was ecstatic and could not take her eyes off the stage even between the acts. Her delicate little hands and feet were quivering, her eyes were full of tears, her cheeks turned paler and paler. And no wonder—she was at the theatre for the first time in her life.

"How well they act! how splendidly!" she said to her papa the police captain, every time the curtain fell. "How good Fenogenov is!"

And if her papa had been capable of reading faces, he would have read on his daughter's pale little countenance a rapture that was almost anguish. She was overcome by the acting, by the play, by the surroundings. When the regimental band began playing between the acts, she closed her eyes, exhausted.

"Papa!" she said to the police captain during the last interval, "go behind the scenes and ask them all to dinner to-morrow!"

The police captain went behind the scenes, praised them all for their fine acting, and complimented Madame Beobahtov.

"Your lovely face demands a canvas, and I only wish I could wield the brush!"

And with a scrape, he thereupon invited the company to dinner.

"All except the fair sex," he whispered. "I don't want the actresses, for I have a daughter."

Next day the actors dined at the police captain's. Only three turned up, the manager Limonadov, the tragedian Fenogenov, and the comic man Vodolazov; the others sent excuses. The dinner was a dull affair. Limonadov kept telling the police captain how much he respected him, and how highly he thought of all persons in authority; Vodolazov mimicked drunken merchants and Armenians; and Fenogenov (on his passport his name was Knish), a tall, stout Little Russian with black eyes and frowning brow, declaimed " At the portals of the great," and " To be or not to be." Limonadov, with tears in his eyes, described his interview with the former Governor, General Kanyutchin. The police captain listened, was bored, and smiled affably. He was well satisfied, although Limonadov smelt strongly of burnt feathers, and Fenogenov was wearing a hired dress-coat and boots trodden down at heel. They pleased his daughter and made her lively, and that was enough for him. And Masha never took her eyes off the actors. She had never before seen such clever, exceptional people !

In the evening the police captain and Masha were at the theatre again. A week later the actors dined at the police captain's again, and after that came almost every day either to dinner or supper. Masha became more and more devoted to the theatre, and went there every evening.

She fell in love with the tragedian. One fine morning, when the police captain had gone to meet the bishop, Masha ran away with Limonadov's company and married her hero on the way. After celebrating the wedding, the actors composed a long and touching letter and sent it to the police captain. It was the work of their combined efforts.

" Bring out the motive, the motive !" Limonadov kept saying as he dictated to the comic man. " Lay on the respect. . . . These official chaps like it. Add something of a sort . . . to draw a tear."

The answer to this letter was most discomforting. The police captain disowned his daughter for marrying, as he said, " a stupid, idle Little Russian with no fixed home or occupation."

And the day after this answer was received Masha was writing to her father.

" Papa, he beats me ! Forgive us !"

He had beaten her, beaten her behind the scenes, in the presence of Limonadov, the washerwoman, and two lighting men. He remembered how, four days before the wedding, he was sitting in the London Tavern with the whole company, and all were talking about Masha. The company were advising him to " chance it," and Limonadov, with tears in his eyes urged: " It would be stupid and irrational to let slip such an opportunity ! Why, for a sum like that one would go to Siberia, let alone getting married ! When you marry and have a theatre of your own, take me into your company. I shan't be master then, you'll be master."

Fenogenov remembered it, and muttered with clenched fists :

" If he doesn't send money I'll smash her ! I won't let myself be made a fool of, damn my soul !"

At one provincial town the company tried to give Masha the slip, but Masha found out, ran to the station, and got there when the second bell had rung and the actors had all taken their seats.

" I've been shamefully treated by your father," said the tragedian; " all is over between us !"

And though the carriage was full of people, she went down on her knees and held out her hands, imploring him :

"I love you! Don't drive me away, Kondraty Ivanovitch," she besought him. "I can't live without you!"

They listened to her entreaties, and after consulting together, took her into the company as a "countess"—the name they used for the minor actresses who usually came on to the stage in crowds or in dumb parts. To begin with Masha used to play maid-servants and pages, but when Madame Beobahtov, the flower of Limonadov's company, eloped, they made her *ingénue*. She acted badly, lisped, and was nervous. She soon grew used to it, however, and began to be liked by the audience. Fenogenov was much displeased.

"To call her an actress!" he used to say. "She has no figure, no deportment, nothing whatever but silliness."

In one provincial town the company acted Schiller's "Robbers." Fenogenov played Franz; Masha, Amalie. The tragedian shouted and quivered. Masha repeated her part like a well-learnt lesson, and the play would have gone off as they generally did had it not been for a trifling mishap. Everything went well up to the point where Franz declares his love for Amalie and she seizes his sword. The tragedian shouted, hissed, quivered, and squeezed Masha in his iron embrace. And Masha, instead of repulsing him and crying "Hence!" trembled in his arms like a bird and did not move, . . . she seemed petrified.

"Have pity on me!" she whispered in his ear. "Oh, have pity on me! I am so miserable!"

"You don't know your part! Listen to the

204 THE TALES OF TCHEHOV

prompter!" hissed the tragedian, and he thrust his sword into her hand.

After the performance, Limonadov and Fenogenov were sitting in the ticket box-office engaged in conversation.

"Your wife does not learn her part, you are right there," the manager was saying. "She doesn't know her line. . . . Every man has his own line, . . . but she doesn't know hers. . . ."

Fenogenov listened, sighed, and scowled and scowled.

Next morning, Masha was sitting in a little general shop writing:

"Papa, he beats me! Forgive us! Send us some money!"

A TRANSGRESSION

A TRANSGRESSION

A COLLEGIATE assessor called Miguev stopped at a telegraph-post in the course of his evening walk and heaved a deep sigh. A week before, as he was returning home from his evening walk, he had been overtaken at that very spot by his former house-maid, Agnia, who said to him viciously:

"Wait a bit! I'll cook you such a crab that'll teach you to ruin innocent girls! I'll leave the baby at your door, and I'll have the law of you, and I'll tell your wife, too. . . ."

And she demanded that he should put five thousand roubles into the bank in her name. Miguev remembered it, heaved a sigh, and once more reproached himself with heartfelt repentance for the momentary infatuation which had caused him so much worry and misery.

When he reached his bungalow, he sat down to rest on the doorstep. It was just ten o'clock, and a bit of the moon peeped out from behind the clouds. There was not a soul in the street nor near the bungalows; elderly summer visitors were already going to bed, while young ones were walking in the wood. Feeling in both his pockets for a match to light his cigarette, Miguev brought his elbow into contact with something soft. He looked

idly at his right elbow, and his face was instantly
contorted by a look of as much horror as though
he had seen a snake beside him. On the step at the
very door lay a bundle. Something oblong in
shape was wrapped up in something—judging by
the feel of it, a wadded quilt. One end of the
bundle was a little open, and the collegiate assessor,
putting in his hand, felt something damp and
warm. He leaped on to his feet in horror, and
looked about him like a criminal trying to escape
from his warders. . . .

"She has left it!" he muttered wrathfully
through his teeth, clenching his fists. "Here it
lies. . . . Here lies my transgression! O Lord!"

He was numb with terror, anger, and shame. . . .
What was he to do now? What would his wife
say if she found out? What would his colleagues
at the office say? His Excellency would be sure
to dig him in the ribs, guffaw, and say: "I congratulate you! . . . He-he-he! Though your
beard is grey, your heart is gay. . . . You are a
rogue, Semyon Erastovitch!" The whole colony
of summer visitors would know his secret now,
and probably the respectable mothers of families
would shut their doors to him. Such incidents
always get into the papers, and the humble name
of Miguev would be published all over Russia. . . .

The middle window of the bungalow was open,
and he could distinctly hear his wife, Anna Filippovna, laying the table for supper; in the yard close
to the gate Yermolay, the porter, was plaintively
strumming on the balalaika. The baby had only
to wake up and begin to cry, and the secret would

be discovered. Miguev was conscious of an overwhelming desire to make haste.

"Haste, haste ! . . ." he muttered, "this minute, before anyone sees. I'll carry it away and lay it on somebody's doorstep. . . ."

Miguev took the bundle in one hand and quietly with a deliberate step to avoid awakening suspicion, went down the street. . . .

"A wonderfully nasty position !" he reflected, trying to assume an air of unconcern. "A collegiate assessor walking down the street with a baby ! Good heavens ! if anyone sees me and understands the position, I am done for. . . . I'd better put it on this doorstep. . . . No, stay, the windows are open and perhaps someone is looking. Where shall I put it ? I know ! I'll take it to the merchant Myelkin's. . . . Merchants are rich people and tender-hearted; very likely they will say thank you and adopt it."

And Miguev made up his mind to take the baby to Myelkin's, although the merchant's villa was in the furthest street, close to the river.

"If only it does not begin screaming or wriggle out of the bundle," thought the collegiate assessor. "This is indeed a pleasant surprise ! Here I am carrying a human being under my arm as though it were a portfolio. A human being, alive, with soul, with feelings like anyone else. . . . If by good luck the Myelkins adopt him, he may turn out somebody. . . . Maybe he will become a professor, a great general, an author. . . . Anything may happen ! Now I am carrying it under my arm like a bundle of rubbish, and perhaps in

IX.   14

thirty or forty years I may not dare to sit down in his presence. . . ."

As Miguev was walking along a narrow, deserted alley, beside a long row of fences, in the thick black shade of the lime-trees, it suddenly struck him that he was doing something very cruel and criminal.

"How mean it is really!" he thought. "So mean that one can't imagine anything meaner. . . . Why are we shifting this poor baby from door to door? It's not its fault that it's been born. It's done us no harm. We are scoundrels. . . . We take our pleasure, and the innocent babies have to pay the penalty. Only to think of all this wretched business! I've done wrong and the child has a cruel fate before it. If I lay it at the Myelkins' door, they'll send it to the foundling hospital, and there it will grow up among strangers, in mechanical routine, . . . no love, no petting, no spoiling. . . . And then he'll be apprenticed to a shoemaker, . . . he'll take to drink, will learn to use filthy language, will go hungry. A shoemaker! and he the son of a collegiate assessor, of good family. . . . He is my flesh and blood. . . ."

Miguev came out of the shade of the lime-trees into the bright moonlight of the open road, and opening the bundle, he looked at the baby.

"Asleep!" he murmured. "You little rascal! why, you've an aquiline nose like your father's. . . . He sleeps and doesn't feel that it's his own father looking at him! . . . It's a drama, my boy. . . . Well, well, you must forgive me. Forgive me, old boy. . . . It seems it's your fate. . . ."

The collegiate assessor blinked and felt a spasm running down his cheeks. . . . He wrapped up the baby, put him under his arm, and strode on. All the way to the Myelkins' villa social questions were swarming in his brain and conscience was gnawing in his bosom.

"If I were a decent, honest man," he thought, "I should damn everything, go with this baby to Anna Filippovna, fall on my knees before her, and say: ' Forgive me ! I have sinned ! Torture me, but we won't ruin an innocent child. We have no children; let us adopt him !' She's a good sort, she'd consent. . . . And then my child would be with me. . . . Ech !"

He reached the Myelkins' villa and stood still hesitating. He imagined himself in the parlour at home, sitting reading the paper while a little boy with an aquiline nose played with the tassels of his dressing-gown. At the same time visions forced themselves on his brain of his winking colleagues, and of his Excellency digging him in the ribs and guffawing. . . . Besides the pricking of his conscience, there was something warm, sad, and tender in his heart. . . .

Cautiously the collegiate assessor laid the baby on the verandah step and waved his hand. Again he felt a spasm run over his face. . . .

"Forgive me, old fellow ! I am a scoundrel," he muttered. " Don't remember evil against me !"

He stepped back, but immediately cleared his throat resolutely and said:

"Oh, come what will ! Damn it all ! I'll take him, and let people say what they like !"

Miguev took the baby and strode rapidly back.

" Let them say what they like," he thought.
" I'll go at once, fall on my knees, and say: ' Anna
Filippovna !'   Anna is a good sort, she'll understand. . . .   And we'll bring him up. . . .   If it's
a boy we'll call him Vladimir, and if it's a girl we'll
call her Anna !   Anyway, it will be a comfort in
our old age."

And he did as he determined.   Weeping and
almost faint with shame and terror, full of hope
and vague rapture, he went into his bungalow,
went up to his wife, and fell on his knees before
her . . . .

" Anna Filippovna !" he said with a sob, and
he laid the baby on the floor.   " Hear me before
you punish. . . .   I have sinned !   This is my
child. . . .   You remember Agnia ?   Well, it was
the devil drove me to it. . . ."

And, almost unconscious with shame and terror,
he jumped up without waiting for an answer, and
ran out into the open air as though he had received
a thrashing. . . .

" I'll stay here outside till she calls me," he
thought.   " I'll give her time to recover, and to
think it over. . . ."

The porter Yermolay passed him with his balalaika, glanced at him and shrugged his shoulders.
A minute later he passed him again, and again he
shrugged his shoulders.

" Here's a go !   Did you ever !" he muttered,
grinning.   " Aksinya, the washerwoman, was here
just now, Semyon Erastitch.   The silly woman
put her baby down on the steps here, and while

she was indoors with me, someone took and carried off the baby. . . . Who'd have thought it !"

"What ? What are you saying ?" shouted Miguev at the top of his voice.

Yermolay, interpreting his master's wrath in his own fashion, scratched his head and heaved a sigh.

"I am sorry, Semyon Erastitch," he said, "but it's the summer holidays, . . . one can't get on without . . . without a woman, I mean. . . ."

And glancing at his master's eyes glaring at him with anger and astonishment, he cleared his throat guiltily and went on:

"It's a sin, of course, but there—what is one to do ? . . . You've forbidden us to have strangers in the house, I know, but we've none of our own now. When Agnia was here I had no women to see me, for I had one at home; but now, you can see for yourself, sir, . . . one can't help having strangers. In Agnia's time, of course, there was nothing irregular, because . . ."

"Be off, you scoundrel !" Miguev shouted at him, stamping, and he went back into the room.

Anna Filippovna, amazed and wrathful, was sitting as before, her tear-stained eyes fixed on the baby. . . .

"There ! there !" Miguev muttered with a pale face, twisting his lips into a smile. "It was a joke. . . . It's not my baby, . . . it's the washerwoman's ! . . . I . . . I was joking. . . . Take it to the porter."

SMALL FRY

SMALL FRY

"HONOURED Sir, Father and Benefactor !" a petty clerk called Nevyrazimov was writing a rough copy of an Easter congratulatory letter. "I trust that you may spend this Holy Day even as many more to come, in good health and prosperity. And to your family also I . . ."

The lamp, in which the kerosene was getting low, was smoking and smelling. A stray cockroach was running about the table in alarm near Nevyrazimov's writing hand. Two rooms away from the office Paramon the porter was for the third time cleaning his best boots, and with such energy that the sound of the blacking-brush and of his expectorations was audible in all the rooms.

"What else can I write to him, the rascal ?" Nevyrazimov wondered, raising his eyes to the smutty ceiling.

On the ceiling he saw a dark circle—the shadow of the lamp-shade. Below it was the dusty cornice, and lower still the wall, which had once been painted a bluish muddy colour. And the office seemed to him such a place of desolation that he felt sorry, not only for himself, but even for the cockroach.

"When I am off duty I shall go away, but he'll be on duty here all his cockroach-life," he thought,

217

stretching. "I am bored! Shall I clean my boots?"

And stretching once more, Nevyrazimov slouched lazily to the porter's room. Paramon had finished cleaning his boots. Crossing himself with one hand and holding the brush in the other, he was standing at the open window-pane, listening.

"They're ringing," he whispered to Nevyrazimov, looking at him with eyes intent and wide open. "Already!"

Nevyrazimov put his ear to the open pane and listened. The Easter chimes floated into the room with a whiff of fresh spring air. The booming of the bells mingled with the rumble of carriages, and above the chaos of sounds rose the brisk tenor tones of the nearest church and a loud shrill laugh.

"What a lot of people!" sighed Nevyrazimov, looking down into the street, where shadows of men flitted one after another by the illumination lamps. "They're all hurrying to the midnight service. . . . Our fellows have had a drink by now, you may be sure, and are strolling about the town. What a lot of laughter, what a lot of talk! I'm the only unlucky one, to have to sit here on such a day. And I have to do it every year!"

"Well, nobody forces you to take the job. It's not your turn to be on duty to-day, but Zastupov hired you to take his place. When other folks are enjoying themselves you hire yourself out. It's greediness!"

"Devil a bit of it! Not much to be greedy over—two roubles is all he gives me; a necktie as an extra. . . . It's poverty, not greediness.

And it would be jolly, now, you know, to be going with a party to the service, and then to break the fast. . . . To drink and to have a bit of supper and tumble off to sleep. . . . One sits down to the table, there's an Easter cake and the samovar hissing, and some charming little thing beside you. . . . You drink a glass and chuck her under the chin, and it's first-rate. . . . You feel you're somebody. . . . Ech-h-h ! . . . I've made a mess of things ! Look at that hussy driving by in her carriage, while I have to sit here and brood."

" We each have our lot in life, Ivan Danilitch. Please God, you'll be promoted and drive about in your carriage one day."

" I ? No, brother, not likely. I shan't get beyond a 'titular,' not if I try till I burst. I'm not an educated man."

" Our General has no education either, but . . ."

" Well, but the General stole a hundred thousand before he got his position. And he's got very different manners and deportment from me, brother. With my manners and deportment one can't get far ! And such a scoundrelly surname, Nevyrazimov ! It's a hopeless position, in fact. One may go on as one is, or one may hang one-self. . . ."

He moved away from the window and walked wearily about the rooms. The din of the bells grew louder and louder. . . . There was no need to stand by the window to hear it. And the better he could hear the bells and the louder the roar of the carriages, the darker seemed the muddy walls and the smutty cornice and the more the lamp smoked.

"Shall I hook it and leave the office?" thought Nevyrazimov.

But such a flight promised nothing worth having. . . . After coming out of the office and wandering about the town, Nevyrazimov would have gone home to his lodging, and in his lodging it was even greyer and more depressing than in the office. . . . Even supposing he were to spend that day pleasantly and with comfort, what had he beyond? Nothing but the same grey walls, the same stopgap duty and complimentary letters. . . .

Nevyrazimov stood still in the middle of the office and sank into thought. The yearning for a new, better life gnawed at his heart with an intolerable ache. He had a passionate longing to find himself suddenly in the street, to mingle with the living crowd, to take part in the solemn festivity for the sake of which all those bells were clashing and those carriages were rumbling. He longed for what he had known in childhood—the family circle, the festive faces of his own people, the white cloth, light, warmth . . .! He thought of the carriage in which the lady had just driven by, the overcoat in which the head clerk was so smart, the gold chain that adorned the secretary's chest. . . . He thought of a warm bed, of the Stanislav order, of new boots, of a uniform without holes in the elbows. . . . He thought of all those things because he had none of them.

"Shall I steal?" he thought. "Even if stealing is an easy matter, hiding is what's difficult. Men run away to America, they say, with what they've stolen, but the devil knows where that blessed America is. One must have education even to steal, it seems."

The bells died down. He heard only a distant noise of carriages and Paramon's cough, while his depression and anger grew more and more intense and unbearable. The clock in the office struck half-past twelve.

"Shall I write a secret report? Proshkin did, and he rose rapidly."

Nevyrazimov sat down at his table and pondered. The lamp in which the kerosene had quite run dry was smoking violently and threatening to go out. The stray cockroach was still running about the table and had found no resting-place.

"One can always send in a secret report, but how is one to make it up? I should want to make all sorts of innuendoes and insinuations, like Proshkin, and I can't do it. If I made up anything I should be the first to get into trouble for it. I'm an ass, damn my soul!"

And Nevyrazimov, racking his brain for a means of escape from his hopeless position, stared at the rough copy he had written. The letter was written to a man whom he feared and hated with his whole soul, and from whom he had for the last ten years been trying to wring a post worth eighteen roubles a month, instead of the one he had at sixteen roubles.

"Ah, I'll teach you to run here, you devil!" He viciously slapped the palm of his hand on the cockroach, who had the misfortune to catch his eye. " Nasty thing !"

The cockroach fell on its back and wriggled its legs in despair. Nevyrazimov took it by one leg and threw it into the lamp. The lamp flared up and spluttered.

And Nevyrazimov felt better.

THE REQUIEM

THE REQUIEM

In the village church of Verhny Zaprudy mass was just over. The people had begun moving and were trooping out of church. The only one who did not move was Andrey Andreyitch, a shop-keeper and old inhabitant of Verhny Zaprudy. He stood waiting, with his elbows on the railing of the right choir. His fat and shaven face, covered with indentations left by pimples, expressed on this occasion two contradictory feelings: resignation in the face of inevitable destiny, and stupid, unbounded disdain for the smocks and striped kerchiefs passing by him. As it was Sunday, he was dressed like a dandy. He wore a long cloth overcoat with yellow bone buttons, blue trousers not thrust into his boots, and sturdy goloshes—the huge clumsy goloshes only seen on the feet of practical and prudent persons of firm religious convictions.

His torpid eyes, sunk in fat, were fixed upon the ikon stand. He saw the long familiar figures of the saints, the verger Matvey puffing out his cheeks and blowing out the candles, the darkened candle stands, the threadbare carpet, the sacristan Lopuhov running impulsively from the altar and carrying the holy bread to the churchwarden. . . .

All these things he had seen for years, and seen over
and over again like the five fingers of his hand. . . .
There was only one thing, however, that was somewhat strange and unusual. Father Grigory, still
in his vestments, was standing at the north door,
twitching his thick eyebrows angrily.

"Who is it he is winking at ? God bless him !"
thought the shopkeeper. "And he is beckoning
with his finger ! And he stamped his foot ! What
next ! What's the matter, Holy Queen and
Mother ! Whom does he mean it for ?"

Andrey Andreyitch looked round and saw the
church completely deserted. There were some
ten people standing at the door, but they had
their backs to the altar.

"Do come when you are called ! Why do you
stand like a graven image ?" he heard Father
Grigory's angry voice. "I am calling you."

The shopkeeper looked at Father Grigory's red
and wrathful face, and only then realized that the
twitching eyebrows and beckoning finger might
refer to him. He started, left the railing, and
hesitatingly walked towards the altar, tramping
with his heavy goloshes.

"Andrey Andreyitch, was it you asked for
prayers for the rest of Mariya's soul ?" asked the
priest, his eyes angrily transfixing the shopkeeper's
fat, perspiring face.

"Yes, Father."

"Then it was you wrote this ? You ?" And
Father Grigory angrily thrust before his eyes the
little note.

And on this little note, handed in by Andrey

Andreyitch before mass, was written in big, as it were staggering, letters:

"For the rest of the soul of the servant of God, the harlot Mariya."

"Yes, certainly I wrote it, . . ." answered the shopkeeper.

"How dared you write it?" whispered the priest, and in his husky whisper there was a note of wrath and alarm.

The shopkeeper looked at him in blank amazement; he was perplexed, and he, too, was alarmed. Father Grigory had never in his life spoken in such a tone to a leading resident of Verhny Zaprudy. Both were silent for a minute, staring into each other's face. The shopkeeper's amazement was so great that his fat face spread in all directions like spilt dough.

"How dared you?" repeated the priest.

"Wha . . . what?" asked Andrey Andreyitch in bewilderment.

"You don't understand?" whispered Father Grigory, stepping back in astonishment and clasping his hands. "What have you got on your shoulders, a head or some other object? You send a note up to the altar, and write a word in it which it would be unseemly even to utter in the street! Why are you rolling your eyes? Surely you know the meaning of the word?"

"Are you referring to the word harlot?" muttered the shopkeeper, flushing crimson and blinking. "But you know, the Lord in His mercy . . . forgave this very thing, . . . forgave a harlot. . . . He has prepared a place for her, and indeed from

the life of the holy saint, Mariya of Egypt, one may
see in what sense the word is used—excuse me . . ."

The shopkeeper wanted to bring forward some
other argument in his justification, but took fright
and wiped his lips with his sleeve.

"So that's what you make of it!" cried Father
Grigory, clasping his hands. "But you see God
has forgiven her—do you understand? He has
forgiven, but you judge her, you slander her, call
her by an unseemly name, and whom! Your own
deceased daughter! Not only in Holy Scripture,
but even in worldly literature you won't read of
such a sin! I tell you again, Andrey, you mustn't
be over-subtle! No, no, you mustn't be over-
subtle, brother! If God has given you an en-
quiring mind, and if you cannot direct it, better
not go into things. . . . Don't go into things,
and hold your peace!"

"But you know, she, . . . excuse my mention-
ing it, was an actress!" articulated Andrey Andreyitch, overwhelmed.

"An actress! But whatever she was, you ought
to forget it all now she is dead, instead of writing it
on the note."

"Just so, . . ." the shopkeeper assented.

"You ought to do penance," boomed the deacon
from the depths of the altar, looking contemptuously at Andrey Andreyitch's embarrassed face,
"that would teach you to leave off being so clever!
Your daughter was a well-known actress. There
were even notices of her death in the newspapers.
. . . Philosopher!"

"To be sure, . . . certainly," muttered the

shopkeeper, " the word is not a seemly one; but I did not say it to judge her, Father Grigory, I only meant to speak spiritually, . . . that it might be clearer to you for whom you were praying. They write in the memorial notes the various callings, such as the infant John, the drowned woman Pelagea, the warrior Yegor, the murdered Pavel, and so on. . . . I meant to do the same."

" It was foolish, Andrey! God will forgive you, but beware another time. Above all, don't be subtle, but think like other people. Make ten bows and go your way."

" I obey," said the shopkeeper, relieved that the lecture was over, and allowing his face to resume its expression of importance and dignity. " Ten bows? Very good, I understand. But now, Father, allow me to ask you a favour. . . . Seeing that I am, anyway, her father, . . . you know yourself, whatever she was, she was still my daughter, so I was, . . . excuse me, meaning to ask you to sing the requiem to-day. And allow me to ask you, Father Deacon!"

" Well, that's good," said Father Grigory, taking off his vestments. " That I commend. I can approve of that! Well, go your way. We will come out immediately."

Andrey Andreyitch walked with dignity from the altar, and with a solemn, requiem-like expression on his red face took his stand in the middle of the church. The verger Matvey set before him a little table with the memorial food upon it, and a little later the requiem service began.

There was perfect stillness in the church. Noth-

ing could be heard but the metallic click of the
censer and slow singing. . . . Near Andrey
Andreyitch stood the verger Matvey, the midwife
Makaryevna, and her one-armed son Mitka. There
was no one else. The sacristan sang badly in an
unpleasant, hollow bass, but the tune and the words
were so mournful that the shopkeeper little by
little lost the expression of dignity and was plunged
in sadness. He thought of his Mashutka, . . . he
remembered she had been born when he was still
a lackey in the service of the owner of Verhny
Zaprudy. In his busy life as a lackey he had not
noticed how his girl had grown up. That long
period during which she was being shaped into a
graceful creature, with a little flaxen head and
dreamy eyes as big as kopeck-pieces, passed unnoticed by him. She had been brought up like
all the children of favourite lackeys, in ease and
comfort in the company of the young ladies. The
gentry, to fill up their idle time, had taught her
to read, to write, to dance; he had had no hand
in her bringing up. Only from time to time
casually meeting her at the gate or on the landing
of the stairs, he would remember that she was his
daughter, and would, so far as he had leisure for it,
begin teaching her the prayers and the scripture.
Oh, even then he had the reputation of an authority
on the church rules and the holy scriptures!
Forbidding and stolid as her father's face was,
yet the girl listened readily. She repeated the
prayers after him yawning, but on the other hand,
when he, hesitating and trying to express himself
elaborately, began telling her stories, she was all

attention. Esau's pottage, the punishment of Sodom, and the troubles of the boy Joseph made her turn pale and open her blue eyes wide.

Afterwards when he gave up being a lackey, and with the money he had saved opened a shop in the village, Mashutka had gone away to Moscow with his master's family. . . .

Three years before her death she had come to see her father. He had scarcely recognized her. She was a graceful young woman with the manners of a young lady, and dressed like one. She talked cleverly, as though from a book, smoked, and slept till midday. When Andrey Andreyitch asked her what she was doing, she had announced, looking him boldly straight in the face: " I am an actress." Such frankness struck the former flunkey as the acme of cynicism. Mashutka had begun boasting of her successes and her stage life; but seeing that her father only turned crimson and threw up his hands, she ceased. And they spent a fortnight together without speaking or looking at one another till the day she went away. Before she went away she asked her father to come for a walk on the bank of the river. Painful as it was for him to walk in the light of day, in the sight of all honest people, with a daughter who was an actress, he yielded to her request.

" What a lovely place you live in !" she said enthusiastically. " What ravines and marshes ! Good heavens, how lovely my native place is !"

And she had burst into tears.

" The place is simply taking up room, . . ." Andrey Andreyitch had thought, looking blankly at the ravines, not understanding his daughter's enthusiasm. "There is no more profit from them than milk from a billy-goat."

And she had cried and cried, drawing her breath greedily with her whole chest, as though she felt she had not a long time left to breathe.

Andrey Andreyitch shook his head like a horse that has been bitten, and to stifle painful memories began rapidly crossing himself. . . .

"Be mindful, O Lord," he muttered, "of Thy departed servant, the harlot Mariya, and forgive her sins, voluntary or involuntary. . . ."

The unseemly word dropped from his lips again, but he did not notice it: what is firmly embedded in the consciousness cannot be driven out by Father Grigory's exhortations or even knocked out by a nail. Makaryevna sighed and whispered something, drawing in a deep breath, while one-armed Mitka was brooding over something. . . .

"Where there is no sickness, nor grief, nor sighing," droned the sacristan, covering his right cheek with his hand.

Bluish smoke coiled up from the censer and bathed in the broad, slanting patch of sunshine which cut across the gloomy, lifeless emptiness of the church. And it seemed as though the soul of the dead woman were soaring into the sunlight together with the smoke. The coils of smoke like a child's curls eddied round and round, floating upwards to the window and, as it were, holding aloof from the woes and tribulations of which that poor soul was full.

IN THE COACH-HOUSE

IN THE COACH-HOUSE

It was between nine and ten o'clock in the evening. Stepan the coachman, Mihailo the house-porter, Alyoshka the coachman's grandson, who had come up from the village to stay with his grandfather, and Nikandr, an old man of seventy, who used to come into the yard every evening to sell salt herrings, were sitting round a lantern in the big coach-house, playing "kings." Through the wide-open door could be seen the whole yard, the big house, where the master's family lived, the gates, the cellars, and the porter's lodge. It was all shrouded in the darkness of night, and only the four windows of one of the lodges which was let were brightly lit up. The shadows of the coaches and sledges with their shafts tipped upwards stretched from the walls to the doors, quivering and cutting across the shadows cast by the lantern and the players. . . . On the other side of the thin partition that divided the coach-house from the stable were the horses. There was a scent of hay, and a disagreeable smell of salt herrings coming from old Nikandr.

The porter won and was king; he assumed an attitude such as was in his opinion befitting a king, and blew his nose loudly on a red checked handkerchief.

235

"Now if I like I can chop off anybody's head," he said. Alyoshka, a boy of eight with a head of flaxen hair, left long uncut, who had only missed being king by two tricks, looked angrily and with envy at the porter. He pouted and frowned.

"I shall give you the trick, grandfather," he said, pondering over his cards; "I know you have got the queen of diamonds."

"Well, well, little silly, you have thought enough! Play!"

Alyoshka timidly played the knave of diamonds. At that moment a ring was heard from the yard.

"Oh, hang you!" muttered the porter, getting up. "Go and open the gate, O king!"

When he came back a little later, Alyoshka was already a prince, the fish-hawker a soldier, and the coachman a peasant.

"It's a nasty business," said the porter, sitting down to the cards again. "I have just let the doctors out. They have not extracted it."

"How could they? Just think, they would have to pick open the brains. If there is a bullet in the head, of what use are doctors?"

"He is lying unconscious," the porter went on. "He is bound to die. Alyoshka, don't look at the cards, you little puppy, or I will pull your ears! Yes, I let the doctors out, and the father and mother in. . . . They have only just arrived. Such crying and wailing, Lord preserve us! They say he is the only son. . . . It's a grief!"

All except Alyoshka, who was absorbed in the game, looked round at the brightly lighted windows of the lodge.

"I have orders to go to the police station to-morrow," said the porter. "There will be an en-quiry. . . . But what do I know about it? I saw nothing of it. He called me this morning, gave me a letter, and said: "Put it in the letter-box for me." And his eyes were red with crying. His wife and children were not at home. They had gone out for a walk. So when I had gone with the letter, he put a bullet into his forehead from a revolver. When I came back his cook was wailing for the whole yard to hear."

"It's a great sin," said the fish-hawker in a husky voice, and he shook his head, "a great sin!"

"From too much learning," said the porter, taking a trick; "his wits outstripped his wisdom. Sometimes he would sit writing papers all night. . . . Play, peasant! . . . But he was a nice gentleman. And so white-skinned, black-haired and tall! . . . He was a good lodger."

"It seems the fair sex is at the bottom of it," said the coachman, slapping the nine of trumps on the king of diamonds. "It seems he was fond of another man's wife and disliked his own; it does happen."

"The king rebels," said the porter.

At that moment there was again a ring from the yard. The rebellious king spat with vexation and went out. Shadows like dancing couples flitted across the windows of the lodge. There was the sound of voices and hurried footsteps in the yard.

"I suppose the doctors have come again," said the coachman. "Our Mihailo is run off his legs. . . ."

A strange wailing voice rang out for a moment in the air. Alyoshka looked in alarm at his grandfather, the coachman; then at the windows, and said:

" He stroked me on the head at the gate yesterday, and said, ' What district do you come from, boy ?' Grandfather, who was that howled just now ?"

His grandfather trimmed the light in the lantern and made no answer.

" The man is lost," he said a little later, with a yawn. "He is lost, and his children are ruined, too. It's a disgrace for his children for the rest of their lives now."

The porter came back and sat down by the lantern.

" He is dead," he said. " They have sent to the almshouse for the old women to lay him out."

" The kingdom of heaven and eternal peace to him !" whispered the coachman, and he crossed himself.

Looking at him, Alyoshka crossed himself too.

" You can't pray for such as him," said the fish-hawker.

" Why not ?"

" It's a sin."

" That's true," the porter assented. " Now his soul has gone straight to hell, to the devil. . . ."

" It's a sin," repeated the fish-hawker; " such as he have no funeral, no requiem, but are buried like carrion with no respect."

The old man put on his cap and got up.

" It was the same thing at our lady's," he said,

pulling his cap on further. "We were serfs in those days; the younger son of our mistress, the General's lady, shot himself through the mouth with a pistol, from too much learning, too. It seems that by law such have to be buried outside the cemetery, without priests, without a requiem service; but to save disgrace our lady, you know, bribed the police and the doctors, and they gave her a paper to say her son had done it when delirious, not knowing what he was doing. You can do anything with money. So he had a funeral with priests and every honour, the music played, and he was buried in the church; for the deceased General had built that church with his own money, and all his family were buried there. Only this is what happened, friends. One month passed, and then another, and it was all right. In the third month they informed the General's lady that the watchmen had come from that same church. What did they want? They were brought to her, they fell at her feet. 'We can't go on serving, your excellency,' they said. 'Look out for other watchmen and graciously dismiss us.' 'What for?' 'No,' they said, 'we can't possibly; your son howls under the church all night.'"

Alyoshka shuddered, and pressed his face to the coachman's back so as not to see the windows.

"At first the General's lady would not listen," continued the old man. "'All this is your fancy, you simple folk have such notions,' she said. 'A dead man cannot howl.' Some time afterwards the watchmen came to her again, and with them the sacristan. So the sacristan, too, had heard him howling. The General's lady saw that it was a bad job; she locked herself in her bedroom with the watchmen. 'Here, my friends, here are twenty-five roubles for you, and for that go by night in secret, so that no one should hear or see you, dig up my unhappy son, and bury him,' she said, 'outside the cemetery.' And I suppose she stood them a glass. . . . And the watchmen did so. The stone with the inscription on it is there to this day, but he himself, the General's son, is outside the cemetery. . . . O Lord, forgive us our transgressions!" sighed the fish-hawker. "There is only one day in the year when one may pray for such people: the Saturday before Trinity. . . . You mustn't give alms to beggars for their sake, it is a sin, but you may feed the birds for the rest of their souls. The General's lady used to go out to the cross-roads every three days to feed the birds. Once at the cross-roads a black dog suddenly appeared; it ran up to the bread, and was such a . . . we all know what that dog was. The General's lady was like a half-crazy creature for five days afterwards, she neither ate nor drank. . . . All at once she fell on her knees in the garden, and prayed and prayed. . . . Well, good-bye, friends, the blessing of God and the Heavenly Mother be with you. Let us go, Mihailo, you'll open the gate for me."

The fish-hawker and the porter went out. The coachman and Alyoshka went out too, so as not to be left in the coach-house.

"The man was living and is dead!" said the coachman, looking towards the windows where shadows were still flitting to and fro. "Only this morning he was walking about the yard, and now he is lying dead."

"The time will come and we shall die too," said the porter, walking away with the fish-hawker, and at once they both vanished from sight in the darkness.

The coachman, and Alyoshka after him, somewhat timidly went up to the lighted windows. A very pale lady with large tear-stained eyes, and a fine-looking grey-headed man, were moving two card-tables into the middle of the room, probably with the intention of laying the dead man upon them, and on the green cloth of the table numbers could still be seen written in chalk. The cook who had run about the yard wailing in the morning was now standing on a chair, stretching up to try and cover the looking-glass with a towel.

"Grandfather, what are they doing?" asked Alyoshka in a whisper.

"They are just going to lay him on the tables," answered his grandfather. "Let us go, child, it is bedtime."

The coachman and Alyoshka went back to the coach-house. They said their prayers, and took off their boots. Stepan lay down in a corner on the floor, Alyoshka in a sledge. The doors of the coach-house were shut, there was a horrible stench from the extinguished lantern. A little later Alyoshka sat up and looked about him; through the crack of the door he could still see a light from those lighted windows.

"Grandfather, I am frightened!" he said.

"Come, go to sleep, go to sleep! . . ."

"I tell you I am frightened!"

"What are you frightened of? What a baby!"

They were silent.

Alyoshka suddenly jumped out of the sledge and, loudly weeping, ran to his grandfather.

"What is it? What's the matter?" cried the coachman in a fright, getting up also.

"He's howling!"

"Who is howling?"

"I am frightened, grandfather, do you hear?"

The coachman listened.

"It's their crying," he said. "Come! there, little silly! They are sad, so they are crying."

"I want to go home, . . ." his grandson went on sobbing and trembling all over. "Grandfather, let us go back to the village, to mammy; come, grandfather dear, God will give you the heavenly kingdom for it. . . ."

"What a silly, ah! Come, be quiet, be quiet! Be quiet, I will light the lantern, . . . silly!"

The coachman fumbled for the matches and lighted the lantern. But the light did not comfort Alyoshka.

"Grandfather Stepan, let's go to the village!" he besought him, weeping. "I am frightened here; oh, oh, how frightened I am! And why did you bring me from the village, accursed man?"

"Who's an accursed man? You mustn't use such disrespectable words to your lawful grandfather. I shall whip you."

"Do whip me, grandfather, do; beat me like Sidor's goat, but only take me to mammy, for God's mercy! . . ."

"Come, come, grandson, come!" the coachman said kindly. "It's all right, don't be frightened. . . . I am frightened myself. . . . Say your prayers!"

The door creaked and the porter's head appeared.

"Aren't you asleep, Stepan?" he asked. "I shan't get any sleep all night," he said, coming in. "I shall be opening and shutting the gates all night. . . . What are you crying for, Alyoshka?"

"He is frightened," the coachman answered for his grandson.

Again there was the sound of a wailing voice in the air. The porter said:

"They are crying. The mother can't believe her eyes. . . . It's dreadful how upset she is."

"And is the father there?"

"Yes. . . . The father is all right. He sits in the corner and says nothing. They have taken the children to relations. . . . Well, Stepan, shall we have a game of trumps?"

"Yes," the coachman agreed, scratching himself, "and you, Alyoshka, go to sleep. Almost big enough to be married, and blubbering, you rascal. Come, go along, grandson, go along. . . ."

The presence of the porter reassured Alyoshka. He went, not very resolutely, towards the sledge and lay down. And while he was falling asleep he heard a half-whisper.

"I beat and cover," said his grandfather.

"I beat and cover," repeated the porter.

The bell rang in the yard, the door creaked
and seemed also saying: "I beat and cover."
When Alyoshka dreamed of the gentleman, and,
frightened by his eyes, jumped up and burst out
crying, it was morning, his grandfather was snoring, and the coach-house no longer seemed terrible.

PANIC FEARS

PANIC FEARS

DURING all the years I have been living in this world I have only three times been terrified.

The first real terror, which made my hair stand on end and made shivers run all over me, was caused by a trivial but strange phenomenon. It happened that, having nothing to do one July evening, I drove to the station for the newspapers. It was a still, warm, almost sultry evening, like all those monotonous evenings in July which, when once they have set in, go on for a week, a fortnight, or sometimes longer, in regular unbroken succession, and are suddenly cut short by a violent thunderstorm and a lavish downpour of rain that refreshes everything for a long time.

The sun had set some time before, and an unbroken grey dusk lay all over the land. The mawkishly sweet scents of the grass and flowers were heavy in the motionless, stagnant air.

I was driving in a rough trolley. Behind my back the gardener's son Pashka, a boy of eight years old, whom I had taken with me to look after the horse in case of necessity, was gently snoring, with his head on a sack of oats. Our way lay along a narrow by-road, straight as a ruler, which lay hid like a great snake in the tall thick rye. There was a pale light from the afterglow of sunset; a streak of light cut its way through a narrow, uncouth-looking cloud, which seemed sometimes like a boat and sometimes like a man wrapped in a quilt. . . .

I had driven a mile and a half, or two miles, when against the pale background of the evening glow there came into sight one after another some graceful tall poplars; a river glimmered beyond them, and a gorgeous picture suddenly, as though by magic, lay stretched before me. I had to stop the horse, for our straight road broke off abruptly and ran down a steep incline overgrown with bushes. We were standing on the hillside and beneath us at the bottom lay a huge hole full of twilight, of fantastic shapes, and of space. At the bottom of this hole, in a wide plain guarded by the poplars and caressed by the gleaming river, nestled a village. It was now sleeping. . . . Its huts, its church with the belfry, its trees, stood out against the grey twilight and were reflected darkly in the smooth surface of the river.

I waked Pashka for fear he should fall out, and began cautiously going down.

"Have we got to Lukovo?" asked Pashka, lifting his head lazily.

"Yes. Hold the reins! . . ."

I led the horse down the hill and looked at the village. At the first glance one strange circumstance caught my attention: at the very top of the belfry, in the tiny window between the cupola and the bells, a light was twinkling. This light was like that of a smouldering lamp, at one moment dying down, at another flickering up. What could it come from ? Its source was beyond my comprehension. It could not be burning at the window, for there were neither ikons nor lamps in the top turret of the belfry; there was nothing there, as I knew, but beams, dust, and spiders' webs. It was hard to climb up into that turret, for the passage to it from the belfry was closely blocked up.

It was more likely than anything else to be the reflection of some outside light, but though I strained my eyes to the utmost, I could not see one other speck of light in the vast expanse that lay before me. There was no moon. The pale and, by now, quite dim streak of the afterglow could not have been reflected, for the window looked not to the west, but to the east. These and other similar considerations were straying through my mind all the while that I was going down the slope with the horse. At the bottom I sat down by the roadside and looked again at the light. As before, it was glimmering and flaring up.

"Strange," I thought, lost in conjecture. "Very strange."

And little by little I was overcome by an unpleasant feeling. At first I thought that this was vexation at not being able to explain a simple phenomenon; but afterwards, when I suddenly turned away from the light in horror and caught hold of Pashka with one hand, it became clear that I was overcome with terror. . . .

I was seized with a feeling of loneliness, misery, and horror, as though I had been flung down against my will into this great hole full of shadows, where I was standing all alone with the belfry looking at me with its red eye.

"Pashka!" I cried, closing my eyes in horror.

"Well?"

"Pashka, what's that gleaming on the belfry?"

Pashka looked over my shoulder at the belfry and gave a yawn.

"Who can tell?"

This brief conversation with the boy reassured me for a little, but not for long. Pashka, seeing my uneasiness, fastened his big eyes upon the light, looked at me again, then again at the light. . . .

"I am frightened," he whispered.

At this point, beside myself with terror, I clutched the boy with one hand, huddled up to him, and gave the horse a violent lash.

"It's stupid!" I said to myself. "That phenomenon is only terrible because I don't understand it; everything we don't understand is mysterious."

I tried to persuade myself, but at the same time I did not leave off lashing the horse. When we reached the posting station I purposely stayed for a full hour chatting with the overseer, and read through two or three newspapers, but the feeling of uneasiness did not leave me. On the way back the light was not to be seen, but on the other hand the silhouettes of the huts, of the poplars, and of the hill up which I had to drive, seemed to me as though animated. And why the light was there I don't know to this day.

The second terror I experienced was excited by a circumstance no less trivial. . . . I was returning from a romantic interview. It was one o'clock

at night, the time when nature is buried in the
soundest, sweetest sleep before the dawn. That
time nature was not sleeping, and one could not
call the night a still one. Corncrakes, quails,
nightingales, and woodcocks were calling, crickets
and grasshoppers were chirruping. There was a
light mist over the grass, and clouds were scurrying straight ahead across the sky near the moon.
Nature was awake, as though afraid of missing
the best moments of her life.

I walked along a narrow path at the very edge
of a railway embankment. The moonlight glided
over the lines, which were already covered with
dew. Great shadows from the clouds kept flitting
over the embankment. Far ahead, a dim green
light was glimmering peacefully.

"So everything is well," I thought, looking at
them.

I had a quiet, peaceful, comfortable feeling in
my heart. I was returning from a tryst, I had
no need to hurry; I was not sleepy, and I was conscious of youth and health in every sigh, every
step I took, rousing a dull echo in the monotonous
hum of the night. I don't know what I was feeling
then, but I remember I was happy, very happy.

I had gone not more than three-quarters of a
mile when I suddenly heard behind me a monotonous sound, a rumbling, rather like the roar of a
great stream. It grew louder and louder every
second, and sounded nearer and nearer. I looked
round; a hundred paces from me was the dark
copse from which I had only just come; there the
embankment turned to the right in a graceful

curve and vanished among the trees. I stood still in perplexity and waited. A huge black body appeared at once at the turn, noisily darted towards me, and with the swiftness of a bird flew past me along the rails. Less than half a minute passed and the blur had vanished, the rumble melted away into the noise of the night.

It was an ordinary goods truck. There was nothing peculiar about it in itself, but its appearance without an engine and in the night puzzled me. Where could it have come from and what force sent it flying so rapidly along the rails? Where did it come from and where was it flying to?

If I had been superstitious I should have made up my mind it was a party of demons and witches journeying to a devils' sabbath, and should have gone on my way; but as it was, the phenomenon was absolutely inexplicable to me. I did not believe my eyes, and was entangled in conjectures like a fly in a spider's web. . . .

I suddenly realized that I was utterly alone on the whole vast plain; that the night, which by now seemed inhospitable, was peeping into my face and dogging my footsteps; all the sounds, the cries of the birds, the whisperings of the trees, seemed sinister, and existing simply to alarm my imagination. I dashed on like a madman, and without realizing what I was doing I ran, trying to run faster and faster. And at once I heard something to which I had paid no attention before: that is, the plaintive whining of the telegraph wires.

"This is beyond everything," I said, trying to shame myself. "It's cowardice! it's silly!"

But cowardice was stronger than common sense. I only slackened my pace when I reached the green light, where I saw a dark signal-box, and near it on the embankment the figure of a man, probably the signalman.

"Did you see it?" I asked breathlessly.

"See whom? What?"

"Why, a truck ran by."

"I saw it, . . ." the peasant said reluctantly. "It broke away from the goods train. There is an incline at the ninetieth mile; . . . the train is dragged uphill. The coupling on the last truck gave way, so it broke off and ran back. . . . There is no catching it now! . . ."

The strange phenomenon was explained and its fantastic character vanished. My panic was over and I was able to go on my way.

My third fright came upon me as I was going home from stand shooting in early spring. It was in the dusk of evening. The forest road was covered with pools from a recent shower of rain, and the earth squelched under one's feet. The crimson glow of sunset flooded the whole forest, colouring the white stems of the birches and the young leaves. I was exhausted and could hardly move.

Four or five miles from home, walking along the forest road, I suddenly met a big black dog of the water-spaniel breed. As he ran by, the dog looked intently at me, straight in my face, and ran on.

"A nice dog!" I thought. "Whose is it?"

I looked round. The dog was standing ten paces off with his eyes fixed on me. For a minute we scanned each other in silence, then the dog, probably flattered by my attention, came slowly up to me and wagged his tail.

I walked on, the dog following me.

"Whose dog can it be?" I kept asking myself. "Where does he come from?"

I knew all the country gentry for twenty or thirty miles round, and knew all their dogs. Not one of them had a spaniel like that. How did he come to be in the depths of the forest, on a track used for nothing but carting timber? He could hardly have dropped behind someone passing through, for there was nowhere for the gentry to drive to along that road.

I sat down on a stump to rest, and began scrutinizing my companion. He, too, sat down, raised his head, and fastened upon me an intent stare. He gazed at me without blinking. I don't know whether it was the influence of the stillness, the shadows and sounds of the forest, or perhaps a result of exhaustion, but I suddenly felt uneasy under the steady gaze of his ordinary doggy eyes. I thought of Faust and his bulldog, and of the fact that nervous people sometimes when exhausted have hallucinations. That was enough to make me get up hurriedly and hurriedly walk on. The dog followed me.

"Go away!" I shouted.

The dog probably liked my voice, for he gave a gleeful jump and ran about in front of me.

"Go away!" I shouted again.

The dog looked round, stared at me intently, and wagged his tail good-humouredly. Evidently my threatening tone amused him. I ought to have patted him, but I could not get Faust's dog out of my head, and the feeling of panic grew more and more acute. . . . Darkness was coming on, which completed my confusion, and every time the dog ran up to me and hit me with his tail, like a coward I shut my eyes. The same thing happened as with the light in the belfry and the truck on the railway: I could not stand it and rushed away.

At home I found a visitor, an old friend, who, after greeting me, began to complain that as he was driving to me he had lost his way in the forest, and a splendid valuable dog of his had dropped behind.

THE BET

THE BET

I.

IT was a dark autumn night. The old banker was walking up and down his study and remembering how, fifteen years before, he had given a party one autumn evening. There had been many clever men there, and there had been interesting conversations. Among other things they had talked of capital punishment. The majority of the guests, among whom were many journalists and intellectual men, disapproved of the death penalty. They considered that form of punishment out of date, immoral, and unsuitable for Christian States. In the opinion of some of them the death penalty ought to be replaced everywhere by imprisonment for life.

"I don't agree with you," said their host the banker. "I have not tried either the death penalty or imprisonment for life, but if one may judge *à priori*, the death penalty is more moral and more humane than imprisonment for life. Capital punishment kills a man at once, but lifelong imprisonment kills him slowly. Which executioner is the more humane, he who kills you in a few minutes or he who drags the life out of you in the course of many years?"

"Both are equally immoral," observed one of the guests, "for they both have the same object—to take away life. The State is not God. It has not the right to take away what it cannot restore when it wants to."

Among the guests was a young lawyer, a young man of five-and-twenty. When he was asked his opinion, he said:

"The death sentence and the life sentence are equally immoral, but if I had to choose between the death penalty and imprisonment for life, I would certainly choose the second. To live anyhow is better than not at all."

A lively discussion arose. The banker, who was younger and more nervous in those days, was suddenly carried away by excitement; he struck the table with his fist and shouted at the young man:

"It's not true! I'll bet you two millions you wouldn't stay in solitary confinement for five years."

"If you mean that in earnest," said the young man, "I'll take a bet, but I would stay not five but fifteen years."

"Fifteen? Done!" cried the banker. "Gentlemen, I stake two millions!"

"Agreed! You stake your millions and I stake my freedom!" said the young man.

And this wild, senseless bet was carried out! The banker, spoilt and frivolous, with millions beyond his reckoning, was delighted at the bet. At supper he made fun of the young man, and said:

"Think better of it, young man, while there is still time. To me two millions are a trifle, but you are losing three or four of the best years of your life. I say three or four, because you won't stay longer. Don't forget either, you unhappy man, that voluntary confinement is a great deal harder to bear than compulsory. The thought that you have the right to step out in liberty at any moment will poison your whole existence in prison. I am sorry for you."

And now the banker, walking to and fro, remembered all this, and asked himself: "What was the object of that bet? What is the good of that man's losing fifteen years of his life and my throwing away two millions? Can it prove that the death penalty is better or worse than imprisonment for life? No, no. It was all nonsensical and meaningless. On my part it was the caprice of a pampered man, and on his part simple greed for money. . . ."

Then he remembered what followed that evening. It was decided that the young man should spend the years of his captivity under the strictest supervision in one of the lodges in the banker's garden. It was agreed that for fifteen years he should not be free to cross the threshold of the lodge, to see human beings, to hear the human voice, or to receive letters and newspapers. He was allowed to have a musical instrument and books, and was allowed to write letters, to drink wine, and to smoke. By the terms of the agreement, the only relations he could have with the outer world were by a little window made purposely for that object. He might have anything he wanted—books, music, wine, and so on—in any quantity he desired by writing an order, but could only receive them through the window. The agreement provided for every detail and every trifle that would make his imprisonment strictly solitary, and bound the young man to stay there *exactly* fifteen years, beginning from twelve o'clock of November 14, 1870, and ending at twelve o'clock of November 14, 1885. The slightest attempt on his part to break the conditions, if only two minutes before the end, released the banker from the obligation to pay him two millions.

For the first year of his confinement, as far as one could judge from his brief notes, the prisoner suffered severely from loneliness and depression. The sounds of the piano could be heard continually day and night from his lodge. He refused wine and tobacco. Wine, he wrote, excites the desires, and desires are the worst foes of the prisoner; and besides, nothing could be more dreary than drinking good wine and seeing no one. And tobacco spoilt the air of his room. In the first year the books he sent for were principally of a light character; novels with a complicated love plot, sensational and fantastic stories, and so on.

In the second year the piano was silent in the lodge, and the prisoner asked only for the classics. In the fifth year music was audible again, and the prisoner asked for wine. Those who watched him through the window said that all that year he spent doing nothing but eating and drinking and lying on his bed, frequently yawning and angrily talking to himself. He did not read books. Sometimes at night he would sit down to write;

he would spend hours writing, and in the morning tear up all that he had written. More than once he could be heard crying.

In the second half of the sixth year the prisoner began zealously studying languages, philosophy, and history. He threw himself eagerly into these studies—so much so that the banker had enough to do to get him the books he ordered. In the course of four years some six hundred volumes were procured at his request. It was during this period that the banker received the following letter from his prisoner:

" My dear Gaoler, I write you these lines in six languages. Show them to people who know the languages. Let them read them. If they find not one mistake I implore you to fire a shot in the garden. That shot will show me that my efforts have not been thrown away. The geniuses of all ages and of all lands speak different languages, but the same flame burns in them all. Oh, if you only knew what unearthly happiness my soul feels now from being able to understand them!" The prisoner's desire was fulfilled. The banker ordered two shots to be fired in the garden.

Then after the tenth year, the prisoner sat immovably at the table and read nothing but the Gospel. It seemed strange to the banker that a man who in four years had mastered six hundred learned volumes should waste nearly a year over one thin book easy of comprehension. Theology and histories of religion followed the Gospels.

In the last two years of his confinement the prisoner read an immense quantity of books quite indiscriminately. At one time he was busy with the natural sciences, then he would ask for Byron or Shakespeare. There were notes in which he demanded at the same time books on chemistry, and a manual of medicine, and a novel, and some treatise on philosophy or theology. His reading suggested a man swimming in the sea among the wreckage of his ship, and trying to save his life by greedily clutching first at one spar and then at another.

II.

The old banker remembered all this, and thought:
"To-morrow at twelve o'clock he will regain his freedom. By our agreement I ought to pay him two millions. If I do pay him, it is all over with me: I shall be utterly ruined."

Fifteen years before, his millions had been beyond his reckoning; now he was afraid to ask himself which were greater, his debts or his assets. Desperate gambling on the Stock Exchange, wild speculation, and the excitability which he could not get over even in advancing years, had by degrees led to the decline of his fortune, and the proud, fearless, self-confident millionaire had become a banker of middling rank, trembling at every rise and fall in his investments. "Cursed bet!" muttered the old man, clutching his head in despair. "Why didn't the man die? He is only forty now. He will take my last penny from me, he will marry, will enjoy life, will gamble on the Exchange; while I shall look at him with envy like a beggar, and hear from him every day the same sentence: 'I am indebted to you for the happiness of my life, let me help you!' No, it is too much! The one means of being saved from bankruptcy and disgrace is the death of that man!"

It struck three o'clock, the banker listened; everyone was asleep in the house, and nothing could be heard outside but the rustling of the chilled trees. Trying to make no noise, he took from a fireproof safe the key of the door which had not been opened for fifteen years, put on his overcoat, and went out of the house.

It was dark and cold in the garden. Rain was falling. A damp cutting wind was racing about the garden, howling and giving the trees no rest. The banker strained his eyes, but could see neither the earth nor the white statues, nor the lodge, nor the trees. Going to the spot where the lodge stood, he twice called the watchman. No answer followed. Evidently the watchman had sought shelter from the weather, and was now asleep somewhere either in the kitchen or in the greenhouse.

"If I had the pluck to carry out my intention," thought the old man, "suspicion would fall first upon the watchman."

He felt in the darkness for the steps and the door, and went into the entry of the lodge. Then he groped his way into a little passage and lighted a match. There was not a soul there. There was a bedstead with no bedding on it, and in the corner there was a dark cast-iron stove. The seals on the door leading to the prisoner's rooms were intact.

When the match went out the old man, trembling

with emotion, peeped through the little window. A candle was burning dimly in the prisoner's room. He was sitting at the table. Nothing could be seen but his back, the hair on his head, and his hands. Open books were lying on the table, on the two easy-chairs, and on the carpet near the table.

Five minutes passed and the prisoner did not once stir. Fifteen years' imprisonment had taught him to sit still. The banker tapped at the window with his finger, and the prisoner made no movement whatever in response. Then the banker cautiously broke the seals off the door and put the key in the keyhole. The rusty lock gave a grating sound and the door creaked. The banker expected to hear at once footsteps and a cry of astonishment, but three minutes passed and it was as quiet as ever in the room. He made up his mind to go in.

At the table a man unlike ordinary people was sitting motionless. He was a skeleton with the skin drawn tight over his bones, with long curls like a woman's, and a shaggy beard. His face was yellow with an earthy tint in it, his cheeks were hollow, his back long and narrow, and the hand on which his shaggy head was propped was so thin and delicate that it was dreadful to look at it. His hair was already streaked with silver, and seeing his emaciated, aged-looking face, no one would have believed that he was only forty. He was asleep. . . . In front of his bowed head there lay on the table a sheet of paper on which there was something written in fine handwriting.

" Poor creature !" thought the banker, " he is

asleep and most likely dreaming of the millions.
And I have only to take this half-dead man, throw
him on the bed, stifle him a little with the pillow,
and the most conscientious expert would find no
sign of a violent death. But let us first read what
he has written here. . . ."

The banker took the page from the table and
read as follows:

" To-morrow at twelve o'clock I regain my freedom and the right to associate with other men,
but before I leave this room and see the sunshine,
I think it necessary to say a few words to you.
With a clear conscience I tell you, as before God,
who beholds me, that I despise freedom and life
and health, and all that in your books is called the
good things of the world.

" For fifteen years I have been intently studying
earthly life. It is true I have not seen the earth
nor men, but in your books I have drunk fragrant
wine, I have sung songs, I have hunted stags and
wild boars in the forests, have loved women. . . .
Beauties as ethereal as clouds, created by the magic
of your poets and geniuses, have visited me at
night, and have whispered in my ears wonderful
tales that have set my brain in a whirl. In your
books I have climbed to the peaks of Elburz and
Mont Blanc, and from there I have seen the sun
rise and have watched it at evening flood the sky,
the ocean, and the mountain-tops with gold and
crimson. I have watched from there the lightning
flashing over my head and cleaving the storm-
clouds. I have seen green forests, fields, rivers,
lakes, towns. I have heard the singing of the

sirens, and the strains of the shepherds' pipes; I have touched the wings of comely devils who flew down to converse with me of God. . . . In your books I have flung myself into the bottomless pit, performed miracles, slain, burned towns, preached new religions, conquered whole kingdoms. . . .

" Your books have given me wisdom. All that the unresting thought of man has created in the ages is compressed into a small compass in my brain. I know that I am wiser than all of you.

" And I despise your books, I despise wisdom and the blessings of this world. It is all worthless, fleeting, illusory, and deceptive, like a mirage. You may be proud, wise, and fine, but death will wipe you off the face of the earth as though you were no more than mice burrowing under the floor, and your posterity, your history, your immortal geniuses will burn or freeze together with the earthly globe.

" You have lost your reason and taken the wrong path. You have taken lies for truth, and hideousness for beauty. You would marvel if, owing to strange events of some sorts, frogs and lizards suddenly grew on apple and orange trees instead of fruit, or if roses began to smell like a sweating horse; so I marvel at you who exchange heaven for earth. I don't want to understand you.

" To prove to you in action how I despise all that you live by, I renounce the two millions of which I once dreamed as of paradise and which now I despise. To deprive myself of the right to the money I shall go out from here five hours before the time fixed, and so break the compact. . . ."

When the banker had read this he laid the page on the table, kissed the strange man on the head, and went out of the lodge, weeping. At no other time, even when he had lost heavily on the Stock Exchange, had he felt so great a contempt for himself. When he got home he lay on his bed, but his tears and emotion kept him for hours from sleeping.

Next morning the watchmen ran in with pale faces, and told him they had seen the man who lived in the lodge climb out of the window into the garden, go to the gate, and disappear. The banker went at once with the servants to the lodge and made sure of the flight of his prisoner. To avoid arousing unnecessary talk, he took from the table the writing in which the millions were re-nounced, and when he got home locked it up in the fireproof safe.

THE HEAD-GARDENER'S STORY

THE TALES OF TCHEHOV

some new book as a library to hire, for instance
about the
...
...
...

THE HEAD-GARDENER'S STORY

A SALE of flowers was taking place in Count N.'s greenhouses. The purchasers were few in number —a landowner who was a neighbour of mine, a young timber-merchant, and myself. While the workmen were carrying out our magnificent purchases and packing them into the carts, we sat at the entry of the greenhouse and chatted about one thing and another. It is extremely pleasant to sit in a garden on a still April morning, listening to the birds, and watching the flowers brought out into the open air and basking in the sunshine.

The head-gardener, Mihail Karlovitch, a venerable old man with a full shaven face, wearing a fur waistcoat and no coat, superintended the packing of the plants himself, but at the same time he listened to our conversation in the hope of hearing something new. He was an intelligent, very good-hearted man, respected by everyone. He was for some reason looked upon by everyone as a German, though he was in reality on his father's side Swedish, on his mother's side Russian, and attended the Orthodox church. He knew Russian, Swedish, and German. He had read a good deal in those languages, and nothing one could do gave him greater pleasure than lending him some new book or talking to him, for instance, about Ibsen.

He had his weaknesses, but they were innocent ones: he called himself the head-gardener, though there were no under-gardeners; the expression of his face was unusually dignified and haughty; he could not endure to be contradicted, and liked to be listened to with respect and attention.

" That young fellow there I can recommend to you as an awful rascal," said my neighbour, pointing to a labourer with a swarthy, gipsy face, who drove by with the water-barrel. " Last week he was tried in the town for burglary and was acquitted ; they pronounced him mentally deranged, and yet look at him, he is the picture of health. Scoundrels are very often acquitted nowadays in Russia on grounds of abnormality and aberration, yet these acquittals, these unmistakable proofs of an indulgent attitude to crime, lead to no good. They demoralize the masses, the sense of justice is blunted in all as they become accustomed to seeing vice unpunished, and you know in our age one may boldly say in the words of Shakespeare that in our evil and corrupt age virtue must ask forgiveness of vice."

" That's very true," the merchant assented. " Owing to these frequent acquittals, murder and arson have become much more common. Ask the peasants."

Mihail Karlovitch turned towards us and said:

" As far as I am concerned, gentlemen, I am always delighted to meet with these verdicts of not guilty. I am not afraid for morality and justice

when they say 'Not guilty,' but on the contrary
I feel pleased. Even when my conscience tells
me the jury have made a mistake in acquitting the
criminal, even then I am triumphant. Judge for
yourselves, gentlemen; if the judges and the jury
have more faith in *man* than in evidence, material
proofs, and speeches for the prosecution, is not that
faith *in man* in itself higher than any ordinary considerations? Such faith is only attainable by those
few who understand and feel Christ."

"A fine thought," I said.

"But it's not a new one. I remember a very
long time ago I heard a legend on that subject.
A very charming legend," said the gardener, and
he smiled. "I was told it by my grandmother, my
father's mother, an excellent old lady. She told
me it in Swedish, and it does not sound so fine,
so classical, in Russian."

But we begged him to tell it and not to be put
off by the coarseness of the Russian language.
Much gratified, he deliberately lighted his pipe,
looked angrily at the labourers, and began:

"There settled in a certain little town a solitary,
plain, elderly gentleman called Thomson or Wilson
—but that does not matter; the surname is not
the point. He followed an honourable profession:
he was a doctor. He was always morose and un-
sociable, and only spoke when required by his profession. He never visited anyone, never extended
his acquaintance beyond a silent bow, and lived
as humbly as a hermit. The fact was, he was a
learned man, and in those days learned men were
not like other people. They spent their days and

nights in contemplation, in reading and in healing disease, looked upon everything else as trivial, and had no time to waste a word. The inhabitants of the town understood this, and tried not to worry him with their visits and empty chatter. They were very glad that God had sent them at last a man who could heal diseases, and were proud that such a remarkable man was living in their town. 'He knows everything,' they said about him.

" But that was not enough. They ought to have said also, 'He loves everyone.' In the breast of that learned man there beat a wonderful angelic heart. Though the people of that town were strangers and not his own people, yet he loved them like children, and did not spare himself for them. He was himself ill with consumption, he had a cough, but when he was summoned to the sick he forgot his own illness, he did not spare himself, and, gasping for breath, climbed up the hills however high they might be. He disregarded the sultry heat and the cold, despised thirst and hunger. He would accept no money, and, strange to say, when one of his patients died, he would follow the coffin with the relations, weeping.

" And soon he became so necessary to the town that the inhabitants wondered how they could have got on before without the man. Their gratitude knew no bounds. Grown-up people and children, good and bad alike, honest men and cheats—all, in fact, respected him and knew his value. In the little town and all the surrounding neighbourhood there was no man who would allow himself to do anything disagreeable to him; indeed, they would never have dreamed of it. When he came out of his lodging, he never fastened the doors or windows, in complete confidence that there was no thief who could bring himself to do him wrong. He often had in the course of his medical duties to walk along the highroads, through the forests and mountains haunted by numbers of hungry vagrants; but he felt that he was in perfect security.

" One night he was returning from a patient when robbers fell upon him in the forest, but when they recognized him, they took off their hats respectfully and offered him something to eat. When he answered that he was not hungry, they gave him a warm wrap and accompanied him as far as the town, happy that fate had given them the chance in some small way to show their gratitude to the benevolent man. Well, to be sure, my grandmother told me that even the horses and the cows and the dogs knew him and expressed their joy when they met him.

" And this man who seemed by his sanctity to have guarded himself from every evil, to whom even brigands and frenzied men wished nothing but good, was one fine morning found murdered. Covered with blood, with his skull broken, he was lying in a ravine, and his pale face wore an expression of amazement. Yes, not horror but amazement was the emotion that had been fixed upon his face when he saw the murderer before him. You can imagine the grief that overwhelmed the inhabitants of the town and the surrounding districts. All were in despair, unable to believe their eyes, wondering who could have killed the man.

The judges who conducted the enquiry and examined the doctor's body said: ' Here we have all the signs of a murder, but as there is not a man in the world capable of murdering our doctor, obviously it was not a case of murder, and the combination of evidence is due to simple chance. We must suppose that in the darkness he fell into the ravine of himself and was mortally injured.'

" The whole town agreed with this opinion. The doctor was buried, and nothing more was said about a violent death. The existence of a man who could have the baseness and wickedness to kill the doctor seemed incredible. There is a limit even to wickedness, isn't there ?

" All at once, would you believe it, chance led them to discovering the murderer. A vagrant who had been many times convicted, notorious for his vicious life, was seen selling for drink a snuff-box and watch that had belonged to the doctor. When he was questioned he was confused, and answered with an obvious lie. A search was made, and in his bed was found a shirt with stains of blood on the sleeves, and a doctor's lancet set in gold. What more evidence was wanted ? They put the criminal in prison. The inhabitants were indignant, and at the same time said:

" ' It's incredible ! It can't be so ! Take care that a mistake is not made; it does happen, you know, that evidence tells a false tale.'

" At his trial the murderer obstinately denied his guilt. Everything was against him, and to be convinced of his guilt was as easy as to believe that this earth is black ; but the judges seem to have gone mad: they weighed every proof ten times, looked distrustfully at the witnesses, flushed crimson and sipped water. . . . The trial began early in the morning and was only finished in the evening.

" ' Accused !' the chief judge said, addressing the murderer, " the court has found you guilty of murdering Dr. So-and-so, and has sentenced you to . . .''

" The chief judge meant to say ' to the death penalty,' but he dropped from his hands the paper on which the sentence was written, wiped the cold sweat from his face, and cried out :

" ' No ! May God punish me if I judge wrongly, but I swear he is not guilty. I cannot admit the thought that there exists a man who would dare to murder our friend the doctor ! A man could not sink so low !'

" ' There cannot be such a man !' the other judges assented.

" ' No,' the crowd cried. ' Let him go !'

" The murderer was set free to go where he chose, and not one soul blamed the court for an unjust verdict. And my grandmother used to say that for such faith in humanity God forgave the sins of all the inhabitants of that town. He rejoices when people believe that man is His image and semblance, and grieves if, forgetful of human dignity, they judge worse of men than of dogs. The sentence of acquittal may bring harm to the inhabitants of the town, but on the other hand, think of the beneficial influence upon them of that faith in man—a faith which does not remain dead, you know; it raises up generous feelings in us,

and always impels us to love and respect every
man. Every man! And that is important."

Mihail Karlovitch had finished. My neighbour
would have urged some objection, but the head-
gardener made a gesture that signified that he did
not like objections; then he walked away to the
carts, and, with an expression of dignity, went on
looking after the packing.

THE BEAUTIES

THE TALES OF TCHEHOV

THE BEAUTIES

I.

I REMEMBER, when I was a high-school boy in the fifth or sixth class, I was driving with my grandfather from the village of Bolshoe Kryepkoe in the Don region to Rostov-on-the-Don. It was a sultry, languidly dreary day of August. Our eyes were glued together, and our mouths were parched from the heat and the dry burning wind which drove clouds of dust to meet us; one did not want to look or speak or think, and when our drowsy driver, a Little Russian called Karpo, swung his whip at the horses and lashed me on my cap, I did not protest or utter a sound, but only, rousing myself from half-slumber, gazed mildly and dejectedly into the distance to see whether there was a village visible through the dust. We stopped to feed the horses in a big Armenian village at a rich Armenian's whom my grandfather knew. Never in my life have I seen a greater caricature than that Armenian. Imagine a little shaven head with thick overhanging eyebrows, a beak of a nose, long grey moustaches, and a wide mouth with a long cherry-wood chibouk sticking out of it. This little head was clumsily attached to a lean hunchback carcase attired in a fantastic garb, a short red jacket, and full bright blue trousers. This figure walked straddling its legs and shuffling with its slippers, spoke without taking the chibouk out of its mouth, and behaved with truly Armenian dignity, not smiling, but staring with wide-open eyes and trying to take as little notice as possible of its guests.

There was neither wind nor dust in the Armenian's rooms, but it was just as unpleasant, stifling, and dreary as in the steppe and on the road. I remember, dusty and exhausted by the heat, I sat in the corner on a green box. The unpainted wooden walls, the furniture, and the floors coloured with yellow ochre, smelt of dry wood baked by the sun. Wherever I looked there were flies and flies and flies . . . . Grandfather and the Armenian were talking about grazing, about manure, and about oats. . . . I knew that they would be a good hour getting the samovar; that grandfather would be not less than an hour drinking his tea, and then would lie down to sleep for two or three hours; that I should waste a quarter of the day waiting, after which there would be again the heat, the dust, the jolting cart. I heard the muttering of the two voices, and it began to seem to me that I had been seeing the Armenian, the cupboard with the crockery, the flies, the windows with the burning sun beating on them, for ages and ages, and should only cease to see them in the far-off future, and I was seized with hatred for the steppe, the sun, the flies. . . .

A Little Russian peasant woman in a kerchief brought in a tray of tea-things, then the samovar.

The Armenian went slowly out into the passage and shouted: "Mashya, come and pour out tea ! Where are you, Mashya ?"

Hurried footsteps were heard, and there came into the room a girl of sixteen in a simple cotton dress and a white kerchief. As she washed the crockery and poured out the tea, she was standing with her back to me, and all I could see was that she was of a slender figure, bare-footed, and that her little bare heels were covered by long trousers.

The Armenian invited me to have tea. Sitting down to the table, I glanced at the girl, who was handing me a glass of tea, and felt all at once as though a wind were blowing over my soul and blowing away all the impressions of the day with their dust and dreariness. I saw the bewitching features of the most beautiful face I have ever met in real life or in my dreams. Before me stood a beauty, and I recognized that at the first glance as I should have recognized lightning.

I am ready to swear that Masha—or, as her father called her, Mashya—was a real beauty, but I don't know how to prove it. It sometimes happens that clouds are huddled together in disorder on the horizon, and the sun hiding behind them colours them and the sky with tints of every possible shade — crimson, orange, gold, lilac, muddy pink; one cloud is like a monk, another like a fish, a third like a Turk in a turban. The glow of sunset enveloping a third of the sky gleams on the cross on the church, flashes on the windows of the manor house, is reflected in the river and the puddles, quivers on the trees; far, far away

against the background of the sunset, a flock of
wild ducks is flying homewards. . . . And the
boy herding the cows, and the surveyor driving
in his chaise over the dam, and the gentleman
out for a walk, all gaze at the sunset, and
every one of them thinks it terribly beautiful,
but no one knows or can say in what its beauty
lies.

I was not the only one to think the Armenian
girl beautiful. My grandfather, an old man of
seventy, gruff and indifferent to women and the
beauties of nature, looked caressingly at Masha
for a full minute, and asked:

" Is that your daughter, Avert Nazaritch ?"

" Yes, she is my daughter," answered the
Armenian.

" A fine young lady," said my grandfather approvingly.

An artist would have called the Armenian girl's
beauty classical and severe; it was just that beauty,
the contemplation of which—God knows why !—
inspires in one the conviction that one is seeing
correct features; that hair, eyes, nose, mouth, neck,
bosom, and every movement of the young body
all go together in one complete harmonious accord
in which nature has not blundered over the smallest
line. You fancy for some reason that the ideally
beautiful woman must have such a nose as Masha's,
straight and slightly aquiline, just such great dark
eyes, such long lashes, such a languid glance; you
fancy that her black curly hair and eyebrows go
with the soft white tint of her brow and cheeks
as the green reeds go with the quiet stream.

Masha's white neck and her youthful bosom were not fully developed, but you fancy the sculptor would need a great creative genius to mould them. You gaze, and little by little the desire comes over you to say to Masha something extraordinarily pleasant, sincere, beautiful, as beautiful as she herself was.

At first I felt hurt and abashed that Masha took no notice of me, but was all the time looking down; it seemed to me as though a peculiar atmosphere, proud and happy, separated her from me and jealously screened her from my eyes.

"That's because I am covered with dust," I thought, "am sunburnt, and am still a boy."

But little by little I forgot myself, and gave myself up entirely to the consciousness of beauty. I thought no more now of the dreary steppe, of the dust, no longer heard the buzzing of the flies, no longer tasted the tea, and felt nothing except that a beautiful girl was standing only the other side of the table.

I felt this beauty rather strangely. It was not desire, nor ecstasy, nor enjoyment that Masha excited in me, but a painful though pleasant sadness. It was a sadness vague and undefined as a dream. For some reason I felt sorry for myself, for my grandfather and for the Armenian, even for the girl herself, and I had a feeling as though we all four had lost something important and essential to life which we should never find again. My grandfather, too, grew melancholy; he talked no more about manure or about oats, but sat silent, looking pensively at Masha.

After tea my grandfather lay down for a nap while I went out of the house into the porch. The house, like all the houses in the Armenian village, stood in the full sun; there was not a tree, not an awning, no shade. The Armenian's great court-yard, overgrown with goosefoot and wild mallows, was lively and full of gaiety in spite of the great heat. Threshing was going on behind one of the low hurdles which intersected the big yard here and there. Round a post stuck into the middle of the threshing-floor ran a dozen horses har-nessed side by side, so that they formed one long radius. A Little Russian in a long waistcoat and full trousers was walking beside them, crack-ing a whip and shouting in a tone that sounded as though he were jeering at the horses and showing off his power over them.

"A—a—a, you damned brutes ! . . . A—a—a, plague take you ! Are you frightened ?"

The horses, sorrel, white, and piebald, not under-standing why they were made to run round in one place and to crush the wheat straw, ran unwillingly, as though with effort, swinging their tails with an offended air. The wind raised up perfect clouds of golden chaff from under their hoofs and carried it away far beyond the hurdle. Near the tall fresh stacks peasant women were swarming with rakes, and carts were moving, and beyond the stacks in another yard another dozen similar horses were running round a post, and a similar Little Russian was cracking his whip and jeering at the horses.

The steps on which I was sitting were hot; on the

thin rails and here and there on the window-frames
sap was oozing out of the wood from the heat; red
ladybirds were huddling together in the streaks
of shadow under the steps and under the shutters.
The sun was baking me on my head, on my chest,
and on my back, but I did not notice it, and was
conscious only of the thud of bare feet on the un-
even floor in the passage and in the rooms behind
me. After clearing away the tea-things, Masha
ran down the steps, fluttering the air as she passed,
and like a bird flew into a little grimy outhouse—
I suppose the kitchen—from which came the smell
of roast mutton and the sound of angry talk in
Armenian. She vanished into the dark doorway,
and in her place there appeared on the threshold an
old bent, red-faced Armenian woman wearing green
trousers. The old woman was angry and was scold-
ing someone. Soon afterwards Masha appeared in
the doorway, flushed with the heat of the kitchen
and carrying a big black loaf on her shoulder;
swaying gracefully under the weight of the bread,
she ran across the yard to the threshing-floor,
darted over the hurdle, and, wrapt in a cloud of
golden chaff, vanished behind the carts. The Little
Russian who was driving the horses lowered his
whip, sank into silence, and gazed for a minute in
the direction of the carts. Then when the
Armenian girl darted again by the horses and
leaped over the hurdle, he followed her with his
eyes, and shouted to the horses in a tone as though
he were greatly disappointed:

" Plague take you, unclean devils ! "

And all the while I was unceasingly hearing her

bare feet, and seeing how she walked across the
yard with a grave, preoccupied face. She ran
now down the steps, swishing the air about me,
now into the kitchen, now to the threshing-floor,
now through the gate, and I could hardly turn my
head quickly enough to watch her.

And the oftener she fluttered by me with her
beauty, the more acute became my sadness. I
felt sorry both for her and for myself and for the
Little Russian, who mournfully watched her every
time she ran through the cloud of chaff to the carts.
Whether it was envy of her beauty, or that I was
regretting that the girl was not mine, and never
would be, or that I was a stranger to her; or
whether I vaguely felt that her rare beauty was
accidental, unnecessary, and, like everything on
earth, of short duration; or whether, perhaps, my
sadness was that peculiar feeling which is excited
in man by the contemplation of real beauty, God
only knows.

The three hours of waiting passed unnoticed.
It seemed to me that I had not had time to look
properly at Masha when Karpo drove up to the
river, bathed the horse, and began to put it in
the shafts. The wet horse snorted with pleasure
and kicked his hoofs against the shafts. Karpo
shouted to it: " Ba—ack !" My grandfather woke
up. Masha opened the creaking gates for us,
we got into the chaise and drove out of the yard.
We drove in silence as though we were angry with
one another.

When, two or three hours later, Rostov and
Nahitchevan appeared in the distance, Karpo,

who had been silent the whole time, looked round quickly, and said:

" A fine wench, that at the Armenian's."

And he lashed his horses.

II.

Another time, after I had become a student, I was travelling by rail to the south. It was May. At one of the stations, I believe it was between Byelgorod and Harkov, I got out of the train to walk about the platform.

The shades of evening were already lying on the station garden, on the platform, and on the fields; the station screened off the sunset, but on the top-most clouds of smoke from the engine, which were tinged with rosy light, one could see the sun had not yet quite vanished.

As I walked up and down the platform I noticed that the greater number of the passengers were standing or walking near a second-class compart-ment, and that they looked as though some cele-brated person were in that compartment. Among the curious whom I met near this compartment I saw, however, an artillery officer who had been my fellow-traveller, an intelligent, cordial, and sym-pathetic fellow—as people mostly are whom we meet on our travels by chance and with whom we are not long acquainted.

" What are you looking at there ?" I asked.

He made no answer, but only indicated with his eyes a feminine figure. It was a young girl of seventeen or eighteen, wearing a Russian dress, with her head bare and a little shawl flung carelessly on one shoulder; not a passenger, but I suppose a sister or daughter of the station-master. She was standing near the carriage window, talking to an elderly woman who was in the train. Before I had time to realize what I was seeing, I was suddenly overwhelmed by the feeling I had once experienced in the Armenian village.

The girl was remarkably beautiful, and that was unmistakable to me and to those who were looking at her as I was.

If one is to describe her appearance feature by feature, as the practice is, the only really lovely thing was her thick wavy fair hair, which hung loose with a black ribbon tied round her head; all the other features were either irregular or very ordinary. Either from a peculiar form of coquettishness, or from short-sightedness, her eyes were screwed up, her nose had an undecided tilt, her mouth was small, her profile was feebly and insipidly drawn, her shoulders were narrow and undeveloped for her age—and yet the girl made the impression of being really beautiful, and looking at her, I was able to feel convinced that the Russian face does not need strict regularity in order to be lovely; what is more, that if instead of her turn-up nose the girl had been given a different one, correct and plastically irreproachable like the Armenian girl's, I fancy her face would have lost all its charm from the change.

Standing at the window talking, the girl, shrugging at the evening damp, continually looking round at us, at one moment put her arms akimbo, at the next raised her hands to her head to straighten her hair, talked, laughed, while her face at one moment wore an expression of wonder, the next of horror, and I don't remember a moment when her face and body were at rest. The whole secret and magic of her beauty lay just in these tiny, infinitely elegant movements, in her smile, in the play of her face, in her rapid glances at us, in the combination of the subtle grace of her movements with her youth, her freshness, the purity of her soul that sounded in her laugh and voice, and with the weakness we love so much in children, in birds, in fawns, and in young trees.

It was that butterfly's beauty so in keeping with waltzing, darting about the garden, laughter and gaiety, and incongruous with serious thought, grief, and repose; and it seemed as though a gust of wind blowing over the platform, or a fall of rain, would be enough to wither the fragile body and scatter the capricious beauty like the pollen of a flower.

" So—o ! . . ." the officer muttered with a sigh when, after the second bell, we went back to our compartment.

And what that " So—o " meant I will not undertake to decide.

Perhaps he was sad, and did not want to go away from the beauty and the spring evening into the stuffy train; or perhaps he, like me, was unaccountably sorry for the beauty, for himself, and for me, and for all the passengers, who were listlessly and reluctantly sauntering back to their compartments. As we passed the station window, at which a pale, red-haired telegraphist with upstanding curls and a faded, broadcheeked face was sitting beside his apparatus, the officer heaved a sigh and said:

" I bet that telegraphist is in love with that pretty girl. To live out in the wilds under one roof with that ethereal creature and not fall in love is beyond the power of man. And what a calamity, my friend ! what an ironical fate, to be stooping, unkempt, grey, a decent fellow and not a fool, and to be in love with that pretty, stupid little girl who would never take a scrap of notice of you ! Or worse still: imagine that telegraphist is in love, and at the same time married, and that his wife is as stooping, as unkempt, and as decent a person as himself."

On the platform between our carriage and the next the guard was standing with his elbows on the railing, looking in the direction of the beautiful girl, and his battered, wrinkled, unpleasantly beefy face, exhausted by sleepless nights and the jolting of the train, wore a look of tenderness and of the deepest sadness, as though in that girl he saw happiness, his own youth, soberness, purity, wife, children; as though he were repenting and feeling in his whole being that that girl was not his, and that for him, with his premature old age, his uncouthness, and his beefy face, the ordinary happiness of a man and a passenger was as far away as heaven. . . .

The third bell rang, the whistles sounded, and the train slowly moved off. First the guard, the station-master, then the garden, the beautiful girl with her exquisitely sly smile, passed before our windows. . . .

Putting my head out and looking back, I saw how, looking after the train, she walked along the platform by the window where the telegraph clerk was sitting, smoothed her hair, and ran into the garden. The station no longer screened off the sunset, the plain lay open before us, but the sun had already set and the smoke lay in black clouds over the green, velvety young corn. It was melancholy in the spring air, and in the darkening sky, and in the railway carriage.

The familiar figure of the guard came into the carriage, and he began lighting the candles.

THE SHOEMAKER AND
THE DEVIL

THE SHOEMAKER AND THE DEVIL

It was Christmas Eve. Marya had long been snoring on the stove; all the paraffin in the little lamp had burnt out, but Fyodor Nilov still sat at work. He would long ago have flung aside his work and gone out into the street, but a customer from Kolokolny Lane, who had a fortnight before ordered some boots, had been in the previous day, had abused him roundly, and had ordered him to finish the boots at once before the morning service.

"It's a convict's life!" Fyodor grumbled as he worked. "Some people have been asleep long ago, others are enjoying themselves, while you sit here like some Cain and sew for the devil knows whom. . . ."

To save himself from accidentally falling asleep, he kept taking a bottle from under the table and drinking out of it, and after every pull at it he twisted his head and said aloud:

"What is the reason, kindly tell me, that customers enjoy themselves while I am forced to sit and work for them? Because they have money and I am a beggar?"

He hated all his customers, especially the one who lived in Kolokolny Lane. He was a gentleman of gloomy appearance, with long hair, a yellow face, blue spectacles, and a husky voice. He had a German name which one could not pronounce. It was impossible to tell what was his calling and what he did. When, a fortnight before, Fyodor had gone to take his measure, he, the customer, was sitting on the floor pounding something in a mortar. Before Fyodor had time to say good-morning the contents of the mortar suddenly flared up and burned with a bright red flame; there was a stink of sulphur and burnt feathers, and the room was filled with a thick pink smoke, so that Fyodor sneezed five times; and as he returned home afterwards, he thought: "Anyone who feared God would not have anything to do with things like that."

When there was nothing left in the bottle Fyodor put the boots on the table and sank into thought. He leaned his heavy head on his fist and began thinking of his poverty, of his hard life with no glimmer of light in it. Then he thought of the rich, of their big houses and their carriages, of their hundred-rouble notes. . . . How nice it would be if the houses of these rich men—the devil flay them!—were smashed, if their horses died, if their fur coats and sable caps got shabby! How splendid it would be if the rich, little by little, changed into beggars having nothing, and he, a poor shoemaker, were to become rich, and were to lord it over some other poor shoemaker on Christmas Eve.

Dreaming like this, Fyodor suddenly thought of his work, and opened his eyes.

" Here's a go," he thought, looking at the boots. " The job has been finished ever so long ago, and I go on sitting here. I must take the boots to the gentleman."

He wrapped up the work in a red handkerchief, put on his things, and went out into the street. A fine hard snow was falling, pricking the face as though with needles. It was cold, slippery, dark, the gas-lamps burned dimly, and for some reason there was a smell of paraffin in the street, so that Fyodor coughed and cleared his throat. Rich men were driving to and fro on the road, and every rich man had a ham and a bottle of vodka in his hands. Rich young ladies peeped at Fyodor out of the carriages and sledges, put out their tongues and shouted, laughing:

" Beggar ! Beggar !"

Students, officers, and merchants walked behind Fyodor, jeering at him and crying:

" Drunkard ! Drunkard ! Infidel cobbler ! Soul of a boot-leg ! Beggar !"

All this was insulting, but Fyodor held his tongue and only spat in disgust. But when Kuzma Lebyodkin from Warsaw, a master-boot-maker, met him and said: " I've married a rich woman and I have men working under me, while you are a beggar and have nothing to eat," Fyodor could not refrain from running after him. He pursued him till he found himself in Kolokolny Lane. His customer lived in the fourth house from the corner on the very top floor. To reach him one had to go through a long, dark courtyard, and then to climb up a very high, slippery staircase which tottered under one's feet. When Fyodor went in to him he was sitting on the floor pounding something in a mortar, just as he had been the fortnight before.

"Your honour, I have brought your boots," said Fyodor sullenly.

The customer got up and began trying on the boots in silence. Desiring to help him, Fyodor went down on one knee and pulled off his old boot, but at once jumped up and staggered towards the door in horror. The customer had not a foot, but a hoof like a horse's.

"Aha!" thought Fyodor; "here's a go!"

The first thing should have been to cross himself, then to leave everything and run downstairs; but he immediately reflected that he was meeting a devil for the first and probably the last time, and not to take advantage of his services would be foolish. He controlled himself and determined to try his luck. Clasping his hands behind him to avoid making the sign of the cross, he coughed respectfully and began:

"They say that there is nothing on earth more evil and impure than the devil, but I am of the opinion, your honour, that the devil is highly educated. He has—excuse my saying it—hoofs and a tail behind, but he has more brains than many a student."

"I like you for what you say," said the devil, flattered. "Thank you, shoemaker! What do you want?"

And without loss of time the shoemaker began complaining of his lot. He began by saying that from his childhood up he had envied the rich. He had always resented it that all people did not live alike in big houses and drive with good horses. Why, he asked, was he poor? How was he worse than Kuzma Lebyodkin from Warsaw, who had his own house, and whose wife wore a hat? He had the same sort of nose, the same hands, feet, head, and back, as the rich, and so why was he forced to work when others were enjoying themselves? Why was he married to Marya and not to a lady smelling of scent? He had often seen beautiful young ladies in the houses of rich customers, but they either took no notice of him whatever, or else sometimes laughed and whispered to each other: "What a red nose that shoemaker has!" It was true that Marya was a good, kind, hard-working woman, but she was not educated; her hand was heavy and hit hard, and if one had occasion to speak of politics or anything intellectual before her, she would put her spoke in and talk the most awful nonsense.

"What do you want, then?" his customer interrupted him.

"I beg you, your honour Satan Ivanitch, to be graciously pleased to make me a rich man."

"Certainly. Only for that you must give me up your soul! Before the cocks crow, go and sign on this paper here that you give me up your soul."

"Your honour," said Fyodor politely, "when you ordered a pair of boots from me I did not ask for the money in advance. One has first to carry out the order and then ask for payment."

" Oh, very well !" the customer assented.

A bright flame suddenly flared up in the mortar, a pink thick smoke came puffing out, and there was a smell of burnt feathers and sulphur. When the smoke had subsided, Fyodor rubbed his eyes and saw that he was no longer Fyodor, no longer a shoemaker, but quite a different man, wearing a waistcoat and a watch-chain, in a new pair of trousers, and that he was sitting in an arm-chair at a big table. Two footmen were handing him dishes, bowing low and saying :

" Kindly eat, your honour, and may it do you good !"

What wealth ! The footmen handed him a big piece of roast mutton and a dish of cucumbers, and then brought in a frying-pan a roast goose, and a little afterwards boiled pork with horse-radish cream. And how dignified, how genteel it all was ! Fyodor ate, and before each dish drank a big glass of excellent vodka, like some general or some count. After the pork he was handed some boiled grain moistened with goose fat, then an omelette with bacon fat, then fried liver, and he went on eating and was delighted. What more ? They served, too, a pie with onion and steamed turnip with kvass.

" How is it the gentry don't burst with such meals ?" he thought.

In conclusion they handed him a big pot of honey. After dinner the devil appeared in blue spectacles and asked with a low bow :

" Are you satisfied with your dinner, Fyodor Pantelyeitch ?"

But Fyodor could not answer one word, he was so stuffed after his dinner. The feeling of repletion was unpleasant, oppressive, and to distract his thoughts he looked at the boot on his left foot.

"For a boot like that I used not to take less than seven and a half roubles. What shoemaker made it?" he asked.

"Kuzma Lebyodkin," answered the footman.

"Send for him, the fool!"

Kuzma Lebyodkin from Warsaw soon made his appearance. He stopped in a respectful attitude at the door and asked:

"What are your orders, your honour?"

"Hold your tongue!" cried Fyodor, and stamped his foot. "Don't dare to argue; remember your place as a cobbler! Blockhead! You don't know how to make boots! I'll beat your ugly phiz to a jelly! Why have you come?"

"For money."

"What money? Be off! Come on Saturday! Boy, give him a cuff!"

But he at once recalled what a life the customers used to lead him, too, and he felt heavy at heart, and to distract his attention he took a fat pocketbook out of his pocket and began counting his money. There was a great deal of money, but Fyodor wanted more still. The devil in the blue spectacles brought him another notebook fatter still, but he wanted even more; and the more he counted it, the more discontented he became.

In the evening the evil one brought him a full-bosomed lady in a red dress, and said that this

was his new wife. He spent the whole evening
kissing her and eating gingerbreads, and at night
he went to bed on a soft, downy feather-bed,
turned from side to side, and could not go to sleep.
He felt uncanny.

"We have a great deal of money," he said to
his wife; "we must look out or thieves will be
breaking in. You had better go and look with a
candle."

He did not sleep all night, and kept getting up
to see if his box was all right. In the morning
he had to go to church to matins. In church the
same honour is done to rich and poor alike. When
Fyodor was poor he used to pray in church like
this: "God, forgive me, a sinner!" He said the
same thing now though he had become rich.
What difference was there? And after death
Fyodor rich would not be buried in gold, not in
diamonds, but in the same black earth as the
poorest beggar. Fyodor would burn in the same
fire as cobblers. Fyodor resented all this, and,
too, he felt weighed down all over by his dinner,
and instead of prayer he had all sorts of thoughts
in his head about his box of money, about thieves,
about his bartered, ruined soul.

He came out of church in a bad temper. To
drive away his unpleasant thoughts as he had
often done before, he struck up a song at the top
of his voice. But as soon as he began a policeman
ran up and said, with his fingers to the peak of
his cap:

"Your honour, gentlefolk must not sing in the
street! You are not a shoemaker!"

Fyodor leaned his back against a fence and fell to thinking: what could he do to amuse himself?

"Your honour," a porter shouted to him, "don't lean against the fence, you will spoil your fur coat!"

Fyodor went into a shop and bought himself the very best concertina, then went out into the street playing it. Everybody pointed at him and laughed.

"And a gentleman, too," the cabmen jeered at him; "like some cobbler. . . ."

"Is it the proper thing for gentlefolk to be disorderly in the street?" a policeman said to him. "You had better go into a tavern!"

"Your honour, give us a trifle, for Christ's sake," the beggars wailed, surrounding Fyodor on all sides.

In earlier days when he was a shoemaker the beggars took no notice of him, now they wouldn't let him pass.

And at home his new wife, the lady, was waiting for him, dressed in a green blouse and a red skirt. He meant to be attentive to her, and had just lifted his arm to give her a good clout on the back, but she said angrily:

"Peasant! Ignorant lout! You don't know how to behave with ladies! If you love me you will kiss my hand; I don't allow you to beat me."

"This is a blasted existence!" thought Fyodor. "People do lead a life! You mustn't sing, you mustn't play the concertina, you mustn't have a lark with a lady. . . . Pfoo!"

He had no sooner sat down to tea with the lady when the evil spirit in the blue spectacles appeared and said:

"Come, Fyodor Pantelyeitch, I have performed my part of the bargain. Now sign your paper and come along with me!"

And he dragged Fyodor to hell, straight to the furnace, and devils flew up from all directions and shouted:

"Fool! Blockhead! Ass!"

There was a fearful smell of paraffin in hell, enough to suffocate one.

And suddenly it all vanished. Fyodor opened his eyes and saw his table, the boots, and the tin lamp. The lamp-glass was black, and from the faint light on the wick came clouds of stinking smoke as from a chimney. Near the table stood the customer in the blue spectacles, shouting angrily:

"Fool! Blockhead! Ass! I'll give you a lesson, you scoundrel! You took the order a fortnight ago and the boots aren't ready yet! Do you suppose I want to come trapesing round here half a dozen times a day for my boots? You wretch! you brute!"

Fyodor shook his head and set to work on the boots. The customer went on swearing and threatening him for a long time. At last, when he subsided, Fyodor asked sullenly:

"And what is your occupation, sir?"

"I make Bengal lights and fireworks. I am a pyrotechnician."

They began ringing for matins. Fyodor gave

the customer the boots, took the money for them, and went to church.

Carriages and sledges with bearskin rugs were dashing to and fro in the street; merchants, ladies, officers were walking along the pavement together with the humbler folk. . . . But Fyodor did not envy them nor repine at his lot. It seemed to him now that rich and poor were equally badly off. Some were able to drive in a carriage, and others to sing songs at the top of their voice and to play the concertina, but one and the same thing, the same grave, was awaiting all alike, and there was nothing in life for which one would give the devil even a tiny scrap of one's soul.

PRINTED IN GREAT BRITAIN BY
BILLING AND SONS, LTD., GUILDFORD AND ESHER